Daniel A. Dombrowski, associate professor of philosophy at Seattle University, has written numerous articles and five other books, including *Hartshorne and the Metaphysics of Animal Rights.*

D0844824

CHRISTIAN

PACIFISM

In the series
Ethics and Action,
edited by Tom Regan

Daniel A. Dombrowski

CHRISTIAN

PACIFISM

Temple University Press

Philadelphia

Temple University Press, Philadelphia 19122
Copyright © 1991 by Temple University.
All rights reserved
Published 1991
Printed in the United States of America

Library of Congress Cataloging in Publication Data
Dombrowski, Daniel A.
Christian pacifism / Daniel A. Dombrowski.
p.   cm. — (Ethics and action)
Includes bibliographical references and index.
ISBN 0-87722-802-7 (alk. paper)
1. Pacifism—Religious aspects—Christianity.
2. Just war doctrine. I. Title. II. Series.
BT736.4.D58   1991
241'.6242—dc20   90-19856
                                        CIP

To Leonard Blostic

CONTENTS

PREFACE

THE TITLE OF this book seems self-explanatory, and to a certain extent it is. Four points of emphasis should be made, however. First, this book differs from others in that it is short; it is meant to be a concentrated defense of Christian pacifism. No other such book exists, as far as I know. Second, this short book is *a* defense of Christian pacifism, not *the* official position of any religious group. Hence the reader should not be surprised at times to find some of the topics idiosyncratic. As will be seen, however, I am not a solipsist. Third, my defense of Christian pacifism is argumentative. I intend the book to be of use to scholars who are interested in strengthening the intellectual rigor of their views or to just war theorists who are bewildered by pacifism as an intellectual stance. I do not know if I should be so bold as to hope to "convert" just war theorists to pacifism, but if this occurs I will not be unhappy. Finally, my defense of Christian pacifism will rely as much on philosophical argument as on theological speculation or exegesis. Once again, I think there is a need for a book with this orientation, to remove the prevalent impression that pacifism's appeal is more to the heart than to the head.

The chapters are arranged in what I hope is a logical order. Chapter One shows in a preliminary way, and this on the evidence of the Gospels, that pacifism must be taken seriously by Christians because Jesus himself was a pacifist. In this chapter I examine the views of Paul Ramsey and Elizabeth Anscombe. Chapter Two suggests why, on the rational criteria of the just war theorists themselves, there are severe problems with just war theory in the twentieth century. As a consequence, many just war theorists now speak the language of "realism" or the "war is hell" view, which suggests that war and morality are mutually exclusive. In Chapter Two I analyze Saint Thomas Aquinas and James Turner Johnson, as well as the sedimentation of just war theory in international law. By the end of Chapter Three it should be clear not only why there are problems with just war theory but also why there are problems with war is hell theory, problems that pacifism avoids. In Chapter Three I make use of Michael Walzer and Richard Wasserstrom, and I criticize Walzer's view, a view that is a combination of just war theory and war is hell theory. Also by the end of Chapter Three one should be prepared to ask the question, Why, then, has pacifism been so unpopular throughout most of the history of Christianity? I try to respond to this question in Chapter Four through a Platonic analysis of the negative effect art has had on Christian pacifism.

Chapter Five is an initial attempt to classify the types of Christian pacifism through a treatment of Gandhi, who understood as well as any Christian what Christian pacifism was all about. (Also in this chapter I treat Martin Luther King, Jr.'s pacifism and the theory of war found in Douglas Lackey.) Although the distinction between pacifism as a duty and pacifism as beyond the call of duty is initiated here, the precise distinctions among the sorts of Christian pacifism are developed in Chapter Six. Also in Chapter Six can be found a precise statement of which sorts of Christian pacifism I am willing to defend and why. I will here make use of the views of Jenny

Teichman. Chapter Seven supplements Chapter Four in the effort to understand why the idea of just warfare is difficult to remove from Christian thought; this supplement will consist in an effort to understand possible future wars. I will rely on Henri Bergson here. The final chapter argues that an adequate defense of Christian pacifism would have to consider the divine attributes, both to discover how just war theorists have inconsistently described God and to see if a consistent description of the greatest conceivable being is possible.

In the Epilogue I analyze in detail two recent defenses of just war theory, defenses that are meant to counteract the effect of the recent resurgence of Christian pacifism: George Weigel, on the one hand, and John Finnis, Joseph Boyle, and Germain Grisez, on the other. The book ends with a brief annotated bibliography of works on Christian pacifism and a list of the works I have used in the development of my theses in this book.

A defense of *Christian* pacifism can escape the charge of parochialism for four reasons. First, the idea that war must be renounced comes to us from Christianity. Peter Brock ably shows that there is no known instance of non-vocational conscientious objection to participation in war, and no recorded advocacy of such objection, before the Christian era.[1] (The personal non-violence in Hinduism and Buddhism was vocational in character in that it was applied in a way analogous to the medieval exemption of priests from warfare. One can be a vocational pacifist and still support the just war theory, as long as others fight.) Second, although after the patristic period only a minority of Christians have been pacifists, between the patristic period and the nineteenth century pacifism was nonetheless confined to those who were influenced by Christianity. Third, pacifism is a characteristic form of renewal in Christianity (as in the Franciscans, the Waldensians, the Quakers, and so on); hence the current interest in pacifism has implications for

Christianity, just as the current renewal in Christianity (as in the period after Vatican II in Catholicism) has implications for non-Christian pacifism.

And fourth, as we will see in this book, Christian pacifists (who can rely both on Christian tradition and on reason) and non-Christian pacifists (who should rely heavily on reason) must now travel along parallel paths. The oft-noted (and oft-criticized, as in the case of Friedrich Nietzsche) influence Christianity has had on the history of ethics is nowhere more apparent than in the ethics of peace and war. As is well known, both Immanuel Kant and John Stuart Mill tried to convince their readers that their ethical systems were the true inheritors of Jesus's teaching.[2] Kant made a special effort to show that *the* philosophical formulation of the Golden Rule was to be found in the categorical imperative. These efforts by Kant and Mill to appropriate Christian ethics for their respective philosophies may or may not be persuasive, but one can only be convinced that both sides in the dispute between pacifism and just war theory have appropriated, explicitly or implicitly, Christian principles.

One of these principles is that each innocent person in war deserves respect. (This is not a principle found in ancient Greek ethics.)[3] Because of the direct lineage between early Christian pacifism and contemporary pacifism (say through the agency of Gandhi or Martin Luther King, Jr.), the current attempt to "repristinize" the church has implications for pacifists in general. And because the just war theory was developed for the first time in an explicit way in the Middle Ages, and was then transmitted to international law (for example, to the Hague, Geneva, and United Nations conventions) through jurists who had read medieval philosophy, getting clear on the Christian just war theory has implications for determining how plausible the moral alternative to pacifism is.[4] As we will see, only war is hell theory has non-Christian roots, but paradoxically this theory has recently been attracting both non-Christians and Christians because of the demise of just war theory. It is because of the common threat posed by war is hell theory that Christian and non-Christian pacifists must travel along parallel paths, such that each could learn from the other about the difficult terrain that all pacifists must cover.

CHRISTIAN

PACIFISM

CHAPTER ONE

PACIFISM:

A THORN IN

THE SIDE OF

CHRISTIANITY

IN AN OLD Charlton Heston movie, *Khartoum*, a Moslem man who has just been introduced to the beliefs of Christianity expresses astonishment when he first reads the Gospels. What surprises him is the apparent tension between the pacifism of Jesus and the Christians he has met, all of whom are fierce soldiers. We might be struck with the same sort of tension when we (re)read the Gospels.

In this chapter I will argue for two claims: that the sort of contrast mentioned above is real, not apparent, and that attempts of Christian theorists to assuage this tension seem doomed to failure. This contrast can be illustrated best by sketching, in a preliminary way, two polar positions: one alleging that Jesus (as a paradigm for the moral person) was a pacifist and the other alleging that pacifism is immoral.

First, the most striking feature of the life of Jesus is his emphasis on love (*agape*); in fact, according to Jesus, the greatest commandment a human being has is to love (for example, Matt. 22:34–40; Mark 12:28–34; Luke 10:25–29). And the sort of love he had in mind was extreme, as it was a love that did not demand love in return. Whereas the Old Law encouraged "an eye for an eye" and "a tooth for a tooth," the New Law (which fulfills the Old Law—for example, Matt. 5:17–20) suggests what seems to be a quite different position. That is, when struck on one cheek by an evildoer, do not resist him, but offer him the other cheek as well; do likewise if this evildoer wants your possessions (Matt. 5:38–42; Luke 6:29). Jesus seems to agree with Plato at this point: Those who perpetrate injustice are harmed more than those who are the receivers of it (for example, *Apology* 30C–D; *Crito* 45C, 54C; also see the *Gorgias*, where Socrates exhibits an intense desire to convince Callicles that one can suffer by doing right, but one can never suffer real harm). In fact, not only are we to suffer the injustices of evildoers; we should love them while they perpetrate that injustice (Matt. 5:43–48; Luke 6:35). Put quite simply, for Jesus the meek and the peacemakers are blessed (Matt. 5:1–12; Luke 6:17–49), not the violent, vengeful, or warmakers.

This was no idle theory for Jesus. His praxis consistently illustrated his teachings. All the Passion narratives exemplify his turning of the other cheek. Peter had completely missed the point of Jesus's teaching when he used the sword against Malchus on the night Jesus was betrayed. He failed to realize that *all* (*pantes*) who draw the sword will die by it (Matt. 26:51–54; John 18:10).

Granted, Jesus was not a political, or even a moral, theorist. But the thrust of his teachings and actions make it clear that when the question of a just Christian war is raised, the burden of proof is on the one who attempts to justify a war and yet claim to be a Christian; the onus is not on the pacifist, if what is meant by pacifism is an opposition to war or violence as a means of settling disputes or an attitude of non-violent resistance to evil.

For the purpose of symmetry let me examine the other end of the spectrum. A good example is offered by A. J. P. Taylor's tour de force, his book *The Origins of the Second World War.*[1] Painted with a rather wide brush, Taylor's thesis can be put as follows, or at least this is how Taylor is usually interpreted: World War I was called the "war to end all wars." In the wake of that terrible conflict arose a whole generation of pacifists and isolationists in England, France, and elsewhere. When Hitler came to power in Germany, little resistance was offered to him by the neo-pacifist and neo-isolationist governments that had the power to offer resistance. By the time resistance *was* offered, Hitler's power had snowballed to such an extent that he could not be stopped short of a second world war. Thus, Taylor is alleged to say, although the primary cause of the war may lie with Hitler and the Nazis, the secondary cause of the war was the failure to use force by those who could have used force. A stitch in time (for example, stopping Hitler's remilitarization of the Rhine) could have saved nine (million or more lives). All of this can be seen more simply in the microstructure: If A (a big brute) attacks B (a ninety-eight-pound weakling), then C (a good, but strong, young person) has an obligation to intervene if C sees what A is doing to B. If C does not forcefully intervene, then B (or anyone else) has a right to claim that C is as unjust, or almost so, as A.

Between these two poles stands the Christian who would like to justify war. On the one hand, the Gospels seem to point, at least in a prima facie way, to pacifism. On the other hand, our moral obligation to defend the helpless seems to point toward forceful intervention, or even war, in certain circumstances. Three general alternatives (to be made more specific later) are open to such a Christian theorist. First, such a theorist can reject Christianity in favor of a supposedly more rational, commonsensical, or forceful theory. Friedrich Nietzsche is perhaps the most extreme representative of this tendency.[2] Christianity, he seems to be saying, entails a meek, pacifistic view of life. And because this view is inadequate (for various reasons), it should be rejected. In fact, Nietzsche notes, few Christians have ever lived up to their ideals anyway; so the honest thing to do is to reject one's Christianity. As he so boldly put the point, the last Christian died on the cross. Second, this theorist could take a different route by embracing fully the pacifism implied and exemplified in the Gospels, thereby rejecting *any* attempted justification of war, whether this justification be offered by A. J. P. Taylor, Nietzsche, Saint Thomas Aquinas, or whomever. Third, this theorist could try to find an intermediate position between these two extremes, a position that holds that the Gospels are not *that* pacifistic and that in certain situations (for example, in the one described by Taylor) war can be prosecuted justly by the Christian.

In that Christians have always been citizens of "this" world, the third alternative has continued to be most popular. In what follows I will examine three formulations of the third alternative. The first is by Aquinas (with attention paid to Saint Augustine), who sets forth the traditional Christian view; the second is by G. E. M. Anscombe, who exemplifies a modern Catholic view; and the third is by Paul Ramsey, who offers a modern Protestant view. In that an exhaustive treatment of their complete theories on war is beyond the scope of this chapter, I will emphasize how they would respond to the dilemma of the Moslem man in *Khartoum*; that is, I will examine their positions solely from the perspective of how they can justify their claims in light of the life of Jesus. A more detailed *philo-*

sophical analysis of the just war theory will be offered later in the book.

That Aquinas had before him the sort of problem I have outlined is shown by his manner of raising the issue of war. He asks, in *Summa Theologiae*, "Is it always a sin to wage war?"[3] The presence of the word "always" (*semper*) in this question suggests that normally war *is* sinful, or, better, the burden of proof is on the person who would like to argue that waging war need not be sinful. And because this is the only question in all of Aquinas's writings that deals specifically with war, the phrasing of this first article to the question should especially be noted.

Before moving to Aquinas's negative response to this question, we should note his proposed objections to his position. The first and second objections receive their support from the Gospels. Jesus is quoted as saying, "All who draw the sword will die by the sword" (Matt. 26:52—a passage that has already been noticed to have given strong support to the Christian pacifist's position) and "I say this to you, offer the wicked man no resistance" (Matt. 5:39). The third objection does not quote any source.

Aquinas initiates his response to these objections by quoting Augustine favorably:

> If Christian teaching forbade war altogether, those looking for the salutary advice of the gospel would have been told to get rid of their arms and give up soldiering. But instead they were told, Do violence to no man, be content with your pay. If it ordered them to be satisfied with their pay, then it did not forbid a military career. (Epistle 138 to Marcellinus)

These soldiers were, in fact, told this in the Gospel (Luke 3:14). Augustine notes that Jesus did not speak these words. Aquinas does not say who did speak them. It turns out that these are not the words of Jesus, but those of John the Baptist. We must be on the watch to see if Aquinas offers any evidence from Jesus's life in favor of his position as his defense proceeds.

Aquinas now isolates three criteria (others follow) for a war to be just. First, war can be just only when waged by the *authority* of sovereign government; that is, no individual or group of Robin Hoods can justly wage war. In support of this criterion Aquinas quotes three sources: Saint Paul, Romans 13:4 ("He beareth not the sword in vain for he is God's minister, an avenger to execute wrath upon him that doth evil"); Psalms 81 (82):4; and Augustine, *Contra Faustum* XXII, 75. Second, just *cause* is required for a war to be just. And a just cause, as Augustine also notes, is one that avenges wrongs. Finally, the right *intention* of those waging war is required; that is, they must promote good and avoid evil. Thus, one can be given legitimate authority and just cause for war and still fight an unjust war if one fights for aggrandizement, or out of cruelty, and so on. Again, Augustine is cited favorably (for example, *Contra Faustum* XXII, 74).

With these criteria in hand, Aquinas responds specifically to the objections that opened the article. To the first objection, concerning Jesus's words to Peter when he used the sword against Malchus, Aquinas offers the following interpretation of Matthew 26:52, relying yet again on Augustine (*Contra Faustum* XXII, 70): What is meant by drawing the sword is to arm oneself and spill blood without command or lawful authority. Therefore, according to Aquinas, Jesus was prohibiting *private* persons from using the sword when he chastised Peter, or at least those who do not have the authority of God behind them.[4] Yet, as has been noted, Jesus quite simply says that all (*pantes*) who draw the sword shall die by it, not that all who draw the sword without legitimate authority shall die by the sword. Perhaps if Jesus and Saint Matthew had read Augustine or Aquinas they would have said something different, but they did not.

In response to the second objection, Aquinas argues that sometimes persons must go to war either for the common good or for the good of their opponents with a type of (oxymoronic) "benign severity," as Augustine puts it (Epistle 138 to Marcellinus). No scriptural evidence is offered in support of this position.

Regarding the third objection, Aquinas makes it clear that one who wages a just war must ultimately intend peace, for as Augustine says (Epistle 189 to Boniface), war is for the sake of peace, and not vice versa.[5] Therefore, one is to remain peaceful even in the midst of war, whatever that means. Also included in Aquinas's response to the third objection is a reference to Jesus's claim that he did not come to bring peace on earth, but the sword (Matt. 10:34). But in the present case, Jesus is doing anything but justifying war. Matthew 10:35–39 makes it clear that the intent of this passage is to show the radical nature of Jesus's calling. As he puts it, "He who loves father or mother more than me is not worthy of me." In other words, Jesus brings the sword to cut the umbilical cord, not another person's head.

Viewing article 1 as a whole, one can see where the force behind Aquinas's position comes from. Clearly he relies on Augustine more than any other source and, to a lesser degree, on the Old Testament, Paul, and John the Baptist. But as specifically regards the life of Jesus, Aquinas comes up empty-handed. His interpretation of Matthew 26:52, as has been seen, distorts the text. And his use of Luke 3:14 and Matthew 10:34 not only distorts the text but also misleads the reader by way of omission.

In article 2 Aquinas asks the question, "May clerics and bishops engage in warfare?" (2a2ae, 40, 2). It may surprise some to find out that he answers negatively. But for my purposes I should note how he treats scripture here. He again relies on Matthew 26:52 and John 18:11, the passages that give Jesus's exhortation to Peter after he used the sword against Malchus. Whereas in article 1 Aquinas had interpreted this incident to signify a denigration of war without legitimate authority, now he interprets it to mean an exhortation to all bishops and clerics. That is, when Jesus says "put your sword back in its scabbard" to Peter, Peter becomes a symbol for all bishops and clerics. Unfortunately, Aquinas gives no indication here why Peter cannot also be a symbol for all Christians, as he was in article 1, which would have forced Aquinas into the pacifist's camp.

In that article 3 is concerned with the lawful use of subterfuge in war, and article 4 with the legitimacy of fighting on feast days, one can see that Aquinas's tracing of a justification for war back to Jesus is only half-hearted. Indeed, most scholars see the real strength of Aquinas's position on war in a passage that does not primarily deal with war at all, nor with scripture. This is the famous passage dealing with the principle of double effect (2a2ae, 64, 7), a principle that Aquinas does not even attempt to attribute to Jesus, even implicitly. I will later treat in detail Aquinas's use of this principle.

G. E. M. Anscombe, in her article "War and Murder," reiterates many of the points made by Aquinas.[6] For example, this prominent philosopher invokes the principle of double effect in support of her attempted refutation of pacifism.[7] But she deals in a more direct way with the relationship between the Old Testament and the New in the matter of pacifism. Regarding Christian pacifism, she says:

> According to this image, Christianity is an ideal and beautiful religion, impracticable except for a few rare characters. It preaches a God of love whom there is no reason to

fear; it marks an escape from the conception presented in the Old Testament, of a vindictive and jealous God who will terribly punish his enemies. The "Christian" God is a *roi fainéant*, whose only triumph is in the Cross; his appeal is a goodness and unselfishness, and to follow him is to act according to the Sermon on the Mount—to turn the other cheek and to offer no resistance to evil.

I will later show how Anscombe misunderstands pacifism, but now it should be noticed what her own position is regarding Christianity as a religion: "The truth about Christianity is that it is a severe and practicable one [religion]. Its moral precepts . . . are those of the Old Testament; and its God is the God of Israel."

There is some truth to Anscombe's position. The pacifist must, to some extent, denigrate the Old Testament view of God. The violent description of the God of the Old Testament, who could even endorse the brutal lex talionis (even if the law of the talon was a humane development in its own day), is a far cry, according to the pacifist, from the message of the Gospels. But the pacifist need not violate the integrity of the Bible as a whole in the pacifist position. All the pacifist needs to do to preserve the integrity of the Bible as a whole is to suggest that the New Law *fulfills* the Old Law (for example, Matt. 5:17–20), which still leaves room to argue for a certain continuity between the Old and New Testaments (for example, both point to a monotheistic God who acts in history), as opposed to a total cleavage between the two. The pacifist can have a cake and eat it too.

But can Anscombe do the same? Granted, she has no trouble in maintaining the theme of unity in the Old and New Testaments, particularly if the last book of the Bible is emphasized, where the bloodthirstiness of God is exhibited once again. She does seem to have trouble, however, in showing the significance of the fulfillment of the Old Law in the New Law. For example, she asks, "Why *must* it be wrong to strike the first blow in a struggle? The only question is, who is in the right?" The pacifist cannot help thinking at this point that Anscombe has misunderstood the life of Jesus. Rather than turning the other cheek when struck, she suggests what seems to be an antithetical position: strike the opponent's cheek *first* if you are in the right.[8] Perhaps the pacifist has a less vivid imagination than Anscombe, but the pacifist just cannot imagine in the mind's eye that Jesus ever would have acted (although Peter did) as Anscombe implies he should have.[9]

Although Anscombe receives the bulk of her support from the Old Testament, she also dabbles in the New Testament. In addition to Luke 3:14 (the exhortation of John the Baptist), Anscombe cites, in a cursory way, two examples from the life of Jesus in support of her position, the only two that she cites.

First, she briefly mentions Jesus's commendation of the centurion (Matt. 8:5–13; Luke 7:1–10). In all fairness it should be noted that Jesus does not chastise the soldier's profession here. But as Anscombe herself notes, he does not commend this profession either. Jesus only commends the centurion's *faith*. The mere associating with a certain type of person does not mean that Jesus advocated or approved of that person's profession; otherwise we would have to say that he approved of prostitution.

Second, she refers to the time Jesus said, "Do not be afraid of those who kill the body but cannot kill the soul. But rather be afraid of him who is able to destroy both soul and body in hell" (Matt. 10:28; Luke 12:5). Anscombe infers from this that God the Father himself is not opposed to justified violence and that he is one "who can *and will* destroy the unrepentant disobedient, body and soul, in hell" (my emphasis).

Two remarks need to be made here. First, Jesus asserts only that God *can* destroy a human being's body and soul, not that

God will. In fact, because this passage is immediately followed by the assurance that not even a sparrow falls without the concern of God, it seems even more unlikely that God could be so brutal in administering divine justice.[10] Second, the context of this passage makes it clear that the contrast Jesus is drawing is between finite power (which has power only over bodies) and divine power (which has power over body and soul). It is hard to see how this contrast can legitimate certain uses of finite power here on earth.

In short, Anscombe's position is plagued with defects. These are especially noteworthy in that Anscombe makes claims that attempt to preclude even the legitimacy of Christian pacifism. Aquinas and Paul Ramsey, though not pacifists themselves, at least indicate that pacifism is a belief consistent with Christianity. This *should* force Anscombe to make even more explicit how one could be a non-pacifist and a Christian at the same time; but she does not.

At first glance there might not seem to be any dispute between Ramsey and the Christian pacifist. He notes that the early Christians were universally pacifists.[11] The first Christians who are known to have been soldiers are not found until A.D. 177. For Ramsey, this early Christian pacifism was, in the main, a consistent deduction from the foundation laid by Jesus. That is, it seems that Jesus, in disarming Peter, "had unbelted every soldier."

Whereas Ramsey allows the pacifist to have a tenable position, his own position, he thinks, is an even more consistent deduction from the foundation laid by Jesus. (That is, he does not attempt to preclude the pacifistic alternative, as does Anscombe.) He notes that by A.D. 403 *only* Christians could be soldiers, thereby bringing about "the Social Triumph of Christianity," not "the Fall of Christianity," as the pacifist would contend. Ramsey's book, *War and Christian Conscience*, is an attempt to bolster the just war theories developed by Augustine, Aquinas, and the like. And Ramsey's strategy in attempting this is ingenious. First, he grants that the Christian pacifist has a legitimate position. Second, he tries to show a *more* charitable, or Christian, position. Ramsey's attempt to develop criteria for the just war is based (as in Aquinas) on moral considerations, but not on direct quotation or citation from scripture, whether in the Old or New Testaments. Rather, Ramsey's theories are deductions from the theme of Christian love, or *agape*. He says:

> The changeover to just-war doctrine and practice was not a "fall" from the original purity of Christian ethics; but, however striking a turning-full-circle, this was a change of tactics only. The basic strategy remained the same: responsible love and service of one's neighbors in the texture of the common life.

This becomes even more clear in two examples that he cites in a later work, *The Just War*.[12]

First, he uses the story of the Good Samaritan for his purposes. He suggests that the work of the Good Samaritan is charitable; but a more efficacious act of charity would be to maintain and serve in a police force along the road from Jerusalem to Jericho to prevent injustice. In other words, pacifism may be a position that can be tolerated in a minority, but because it is only an "ambulance theory of Christian charity" it is inadequate.

The second example that acts as a helpful pedagogical aid in illustrating Ramsey's position is his use of Luke 14:28–33. Here Jesus says:

> For which of you desiring to build a tower, does not first sit down and count the cost? . . . Or what king, going to encounter another king in war, will not sit down first and take counsel whether he is able with ten thousand to

> meet him with twenty thousand? . . . So therefore who-
> ever of you does not renounce all that he has cannot be my
> disciple.

In other words, in order to measure what it will take to lead
a truly charitable life, we will have to include the costs of a
police force (that is, an army), which will be needed to patrol
the Jericho roads of this world.

What makes this theory ingenious is that it seems to go to
the heart of the Gospels, which Aquinas and Anscombe failed
to do. But the pacifist, while grateful for Ramsey's admission
that pacifism is a consistent deduction from the foundation
laid by Jesus, would probably find this small solace, affirm-
ing, as the pacifist does, that pacifism is more consistent with
the life of Jesus (or a life of *agape*) than non-pacifism, or perhaps even that non-pacifism is inconsistent with a life led in
imitation of Jesus.

Five points need to be made concerning Ramsey's position.
First, it is hard to see how the change from pacifism to "just"
war theory in the early centuries of Christianity was only a
change of tactics, and not a change in fundamental strategy.
Second, Ramsey does not even attempt to trace his version
of Christianity back to Christ's life. Third, Peter was doing
exactly what Ramsey suggests we do in establishing this police
force when he took up the sword, but Jesus disarmed him.
Fourth, by advocating taking up arms Ramsey has perhaps re-
verted to Anscombe's exhortation to strike first (or be prepared
to strike first) if we are in the right against our opponent. And,
finally, if this is not what Ramsey intends, then he must at
least be claiming that when struck on one cheek (or when an
innocent person is struck on one cheek) we should strike our
opponent back (or at least disarm him of his ability to strike
us, or his ability to strike the innocent person whom we are
in a position to defend). But if this is the case, then Ramsey

seems to disagree with the simplicity of Jesus's exhortation to turn the other cheek. The person who strikes, it will be remembered, seems to be harmed more than the one struck; that is, those who strike "know not what they do."

Although Ramsey at least tries to make his theory consistent with the notion of *agape* in the New Testament (which neither Aquinas nor Anscombe took great pains to do), his attempt seems foundationless in that he does not show the compatibility between his expression of *agape* and Jesus's expression of *agape*. Therefore, all the theories and subtleties of Ramsey's two well-written books are finely built castles, albeit made of sand.

Perhaps it will be argued that Aquinas, Anscombe, and Ramsey could have supplied the evidence from the life of Jesus to support their positions if they had wanted to, but did not choose to do so. One begins to see how the dominant theme of the Gospels, that is, love, plays havoc on those who would claim to be Christians and yet try to justify war. These people search everywhere for an aperture, however small, to see Jesus qualifying his pacifistic exhortations in favor of a just war. Let me therefore examine some of the more likely examples that could be proposed. The first that comes to mind is the story of Jesus cleansing the temple, but this is such an important case that I will treat it with special care later in the book.

Some notice that Jesus says, "But when you hear of wars and insurrections, do not be terrified; these things must first come to pass, but the end will not be at once" (Luke 21:9). Three things should be noted here. First, even if there must be wars, there is nothing here that makes them legitimate. Second, even if there must be wars, there is no exhortation here for Christians to fight them. Finally, whatever is meant by "must" here, Jesus's prediction of more wars before the end (*telos*) is not meant as an anticipation of something that must inexorably draw in all bystanders due to some sort of logical necessity (*dei gar tauta genesthai proton*). In fact, Jesus makes it clear that his followers will have to avoid being drawn into such calamities if they want to be saved (Luke 21:10–19).

Others point to Jesus when he said, "Let him who has no sword sell his tunic and buy one" (Luke 22:36). But the careful reader will notice that these words are said just before Jesus's arrest, when Jesus makes it clear (Luke 22:51) that the "sword" he talks of is not made of metal, but of faith and courage.

As a last straw, some grasp at Jesus's tribute to Caesar (Matt. 22:15–22; Mark 12:13–17; Luke 20:20–26). If taken literally, this passage only gives a coin to Caesar, not one's ability to fight. And whatever the symbolism of this passage exactly means, which is difficult to determine, there is no indication on Jesus's part that it conflicts with what he has said before. It should be noted that Jesus deals with Caesar here only because certain individuals tried to trick him into saying something that he would regret. But Jesus was not tricked into giving Caesar more than was his to receive.

As Thomas Kuhn has shown so well, an interpretation of something often becomes so dominant that it becomes matter of fact, and received by generations of scholars in an unquestioned way.[13] In a sense this is beneficial, for it tends to stabilize the dizzying swirl of myriad opinions and isolate a few important questions for consideration. But at times this is a dangerous situation, for it can easily lead to a smug prejudice in favor of the "received" view. That is, to assume that what has been received in a widely accepted view has been shown to be a worthwhile stance may unjustly discredit a position that swims in the other direction.

Such is the case as regards Christianity and pacifism. Although this chapter has not attempted an exhaustive analysis of the problems inherent in a Christian attempt to justify war, it has sought to cast doubt on the consistency of the claim that the justification of war can be compatible with Christianity, *if* what is meant by Christianity is a way of life led in the image of Jesus. Nor has this chapter attempted to appropriate the Gospels exclusively for the cause of pacifism. For example, Jesus's words at Matthew 5:38–42 may be even more radical than I have indicated above, in that he may have been opposed to *any* resistance to evil, violent or otherwise. If it is true that no contemporary theory can ever completely appropriate the astringency of Jesus's words to the crowds who followed him regarding how to respond to evil, it is nonetheless also true, as I will demonstrate, that pacifism does a better job of this than other theories.

CHAPTER TWO

THE PRAGMATIC

DEATH OF THE

JUST WAR

THEORY

WITH THE PRELIMINARY chapter as a background, a chapter that blended biblical exegesis and initial criticisms of some just war theorists, I am now in position to analyze the just war theory in detail.

There have only been two real options in the history of Christianity regarding thought about war: pacifism and the just war theory. I think at least two points can be made concerning these options on the evidence I have supplied in Chapter One. First, the burden of proof is on the just war theorist. This perhaps conflicts with common sense, which sees pacifism as the odd position in need of explanation. But the pacifist has the life of Jesus, the paradigmatic pacifist,[1] to rely on, as well as the reluctant admissions of Aquinas and Ramsey that pacifism has a prima facie stability within the tradition. Second, just war theorists—including some of the most brilliant Christian minds in recent history, Anscombe and Ramsey— deliver more promissory notes than real arguments in favor of their position.

It might be objected, however, that I can only make my second point by a contraction of vision so myopically narrow that the just war theorist's luster could not possibly be seen. That is, in Chapter One I insisted that the just war theorist could not make a case upon the foundation of the life of Jesus. But Christianity, it might be objected, has never, at least at its best, been slavishly attached to the conditions peculiar to a first-century Roman colony. Opponents to Christian pacifism might note that all Jesus's disciples were Jews, but this does not mean that henceforth all Christian clerics must be Jews first. So also, Jesus may have been a pacifist, but that fact *simpliciter* does not mean that all Christians must be pacifists.

Three comments are in order. First, I am certainly not insisting on anything like a biblical "fundamentalism" in this book; my claim is that the centrality of *agape* and non-violence in the Gospels sets a standard against which Christians who are not pacifists must contend. Second, my method can more accurately be described as one of logical exhaustion. If these (or their variants) are the only two real alternatives to choose from, and if one of them is weak in its linkage to the life of Jesus *and* is internally inconsistent, then the other view that is strong in its linkage to the life of Jesus and is at least logically consistent is the more rational one to adopt. Finally, the just war theory *does* exhibit inconsistencies *on its own criteria*. This will be the thrust of this chapter. That is, quite apart from pacifistic criticisms of the just war theory reliant on considerations of *agape* and Jesus, the criteria the just war theorists themselves have established can no longer be met, in some instances, or have not historically been met in others.

My thesis in this chapter is that the theory commonly designated as the "Christian just war theory" is practically dead. This obituary should have been written at least forty years ago after Dresden and Hiroshima. The closest thing to an epitaph was given by Warren Steinkraus in 1974 when he suggested that the expression "just war" is unintelligible, it is "just nonsense."[2] Eventually in this chapter I will treat the most important living defender of the just war theory as well as the American Catholic bishops' statement on war.

The just war theory was once alive and well. It was born (within Christianity, at least, ignoring classical predecessors to the theory) in the patristic era, and not before. The earliest Christians were pacifists, as has been noted, and not only because the Romans did not want them as soldiers. Their pacifism made sense in that Jesus himself was a pacifist. But with the decline of the Roman empire, Christian leaders found themselves in a schizophrenic position, with one eye on Jesus's unbelting of Peter and Jesus's own non-violence and the other eye on all the real estate scattered throughout the empire. In order to rule such land and defend the people on it, Christian leaders came to the conclusion that they would have to forcefully defend themselves against barbarians. Hence, just war theory was born; no Caesarian section was needed, as it was a smooth birth indeed.

What distinguished the Christian notion of warfare from that of the barbarians was the harness placed upon Christian warriors. It has been seen that the *éminence grise* of the just war theory, Saint Thomas Aquinas, defends the just war as the exception to the rule. The virile manhood of the theory occurred when all the restrictions placed upon the just warrior could be met with equanimity: A just war needed *jus ad*

bellum, or a just cause to fight for, as in the protection of innocent life, and it needed *jus in bello*, or justice performed in the
conduct of the war itself. Paramount among concerns relating
to *jus in bello* was the prohibition against killing innocent
people, a restriction that did not seem too bothersome in an
age of spears and arrows (although sieges threatened innocents
even in the Middle Ages). It is this seemingly harmless restriction, however, that eventually, for all practical purposes, kills
the beast.

Just ad bellum and *jus in bello* are related. A just cause consists, according to Aquinas in *Summa Theologiae*, in a defense
against those who can be killed because they deserve to be
punished for some wrong they have done.[3] At least on these
prima facie grounds, Aquinas seems to be morally opposed to
the killing of innocents in war. Further analysis of Aquinas's
writings bears this conclusion out. Later (2a2ae, 64, 6) Aquinas
asks, "Is it ever permissible to kill an innocent person?" Once
again, the very way he asks the question shows that he wants
the just war to be kept within precise limits.[4] His answer is
quite explicit: "There is, therefore, simply no justification for
taking the life of an innocent person" (*Et ideo nullo modo licet
occidere innocentum*). The only possible exception to this rule
would be the one who might kill the innocent in obedience to
God's command, as Abraham. But Aquinas makes it clear that
this person is not really an exception to the rule, because the
responsibility for such killing would be with God, not with the
person who obeys God. I will return to this morally inferior
notion of God later. At another point (1a2ae, 105, 3) Aquinas
makes a similar contention: moderation should be shown in
war by sparing women, children, and fruit trees (so as to avoid
starving the civilian population). Once again, the only possible exception (which is not really an exception) would be if
God commanded us to annihilate a city as part of *God's* divine
justice (see Deut. 9:1–5).

Some just war theorists try to legitimate the killing of innocents in war by invoking the famous (or infamous) principle of
double effect. It should be realized, however, that there are no
grounds in Aquinas for using this principle in this particular
connection. Some might say the following: "In war one intends to avenge wrongdoing, and although one might not *want*
to kill innocents, one may *have* to do so nonetheless as an
indirect effect of one's actions in a just war." Aquinas never
says anything like this at all. What he suggests (2a2ae, 64, 7)
is that a single act may have two effects: one intended and
one incidental to that intention. The example he cites is of
great importance. Self-defense has two effects: One intends to
save one's life or to avenge wrongdoing, and one may unintentionally kill the attacker in the process. (Although this killing
is unintentional, it may nonetheless be foreseen.) The precise
meaning of "intention" here is not my concern; enough ink has
been spilled already on the difficulties in conceiving an event
that one brings about as foreseeable but not intended. What *is*
of concern is the realization that it is the attacker (*invadentis*)
who may legitimately be killed. That is, there is no indication
that the principle of double effect can be used to justify the
killing of innocents, especially since Aquinas has previously
argued against the killing of innocents, even in a war with a
just cause.

A possible substitute for the just war theory will be considered in the next chapter; I will call it here the "necessary war
theory" (that is, war may be necessary for survival, even war in
which innocents are killed or threatened with death). But so-
called necessity is not the same as justice. If justice is defined
in a preliminary way (as it has been from Plato to Aquinas to
Kant to John Rawls) as rendering to *each* its due, then no killing
of an innocent can ever be considered just from the perspective of the innocent person killed, although the rationalizing
killer may feel "justified" in killing innocents for reasons quite

apart from the rendering of what is due to each person. I am assuming, however, that a Christian theory of justice would have to include the claims of each person, including innocents. Granted, determining exactly who is an innocent person (or better, a non-combatant) may be more difficult now than in the Middle Ages, but the task is far from impossible. Once again, the question of where the burden of proof lies is crucial.[5] "Innocent until proven guilty" has traditionally been the assumption of the just war theorists themselves. Those in the military forfeit their innocence, obviously enough (and sadly enough if they are conscripted under duress), and perhaps also those who directly aid the war effort (for example, in munitions factories). But those who only indirectly aid the war effort by performing tasks that would have to be performed in peacetime as well (growing wheat, delivering mail) surely do not sacrifice their non-combatant status, nor perhaps their status as innocents. This applies even more to pacifists, children, the mentally enfeebled, non-human animals, and so on. They do not receive *their* due if killed in war. Surely there are tens of millions of innocents, perhaps more, in the Soviet Union alone.

The hardening of the arteries of the just war theory set in when technological developments made it difficult not to kill innocents in war. The twentieth century has witnessed a startling growth in instruments of torture and death specifically designed to be used against innocents, with no end to the process in sight.

My purpose is not the histrionic one of describing in detail how cruel it is to burn babies; nor is it to suggest that the people who have supported policies that led to the burning of babies have enjoyed doing so. Rather, I am suggesting that in a world where the killing of innocents (or threatening to kill innocents) is taken for granted, the just war theory has for all practical purposes died. The logic of my position in this chapter is quite simple:

1. Christian just war theory, of which Aquinas is the prime example, has considered killing, or threatening to kill, innocents as illegitimate.
2. Modern warfare *depends* on weapons that either kill or threaten to kill innocent persons.
3. Therefore, one cannot use the Christian just war theory to justify the construction and/or use of weapons that kill or threaten to kill innocent persons.

Nuclear weapons immediately come to mind, as do devices in chemical/biological warfare, which all exist in profusion. But my claim cuts deeper than these obvious cases. If the logic of my argument holds, it holds for most "conventional" modern wars as well, affecting our judgments concerning the saturation bombing of English, French, Japanese, Chinese, and German cities in the second world war, the devices used in the blockade of Germany at the end of the first world war and in the siege of Leningrad in the second world war, the defoliants used in Vietnam to starve out civilian populations (N.B. Aquinas's fruit trees), the bombs dropped on hospitals in Vietnam, and so on. The list is enormous, and quite cosmopolitan. The Russians murdered Poles in Katyn Forest, just as the Turks murdered defenseless Armenians locked in cages.

Has there been a just war in this century? I cannot think of a single one that clearly exhibits both *jus ad bellum* and *jus in bello*. The latter is honored more in the breach than in the observance. The former is sometimes found, but unfortunately not often enough in those cases where *jus in bello* apparently obtains, as in the British fight in the Falklands. If a just war is to be found, it is only in these minor fights, but in the Falklands-Malvinas case *jus ad bellum* can only be established on the Hobbesian right to defend an empire, hardly a paradigmatic example. It is ironic that the pacifist is often criticized for being impractical. My reply: If one cannot produce an example of just war in a century full of wars then what are we to *do* with the just war theory? On pragmatic grounds is it not useless? Some would say it can function as an ideal, but here an egregious category mistake appears. The just war theory is not and never has been an ideal, even on the reasoning of just war theorists themselves, but an instrument to reach an ideal. Peace is that ideal, and whatever value war has is instrumental to it. Augustine, Aquinas, and their epigoni are clear on that point. But if war does not carry with it justice as an instrument, then it even loses its ancillary status from a moral point of view.

An analogy will help elaborate the point I am trying to make from another angle. Imagine a Mr. A, who owns a shiny new Mercedes. He parks his car in front of his house every night before his neighbor, Mr. B, comes home. Mr. B, who owns a battered old pickup, repeatedly dents the Mercedes because he refuses to parallel park in a careful manner. Surely Mr. A would have a legitimate end in mind if he tried to prevent Mr. B from denting the Mercedes. But just as surely, Mr. A's end does not justify *any* means. For example, if Mr. A took Mr. B's child and tied her to the bumper of the Mercedes, he would obtain his end, for Mr. B would not want to dent his own child, even with an old pickup.[6] But in the process of saving his car, Mr. A would have acted immorally by treating the little girl as a means only to his end, albeit a legitimate end. Granted, Mr. B is reprehensible, but that is not his daughter's fault.

Now to the other half of the analogy. Imagine Nation X confronted by Nation Y, which is led, for the sake of argument, by the most vile and perfidious of leaders. If Nation X wants to oppose Nation Y it would seem that Nation X would have a legitimate end in mind, just as in the previous example it would have been legitimate for Mr. A to protect his car. However, if Nation X threatens to kill innocent people in Nation Y in order to hold the evil intentions of the leaders of Nation Y in check, it seems that Nation X is just as immoral as Mr. A was in the previous example. Or more precisely, the people in Nation X who supported such threats are immoral. Treating innocent people of Nation Y as means only to an end, albeit a legitimate end, is immoral according to just war theory. If just war theorists hesitate here, it is with their own theory that they have reservations, as well they might. For even if the rulers of Nation Y are satanic, as I have stipulated for the sake of argument, these innocent people are not to blame.

To get directly to the point, the latter half of this analogy is symbolic of the moral dilemma concerning nuclear armaments. The very willingness to make nuclear arms, much less use them, shows a willingness to use people as means only to an end. It should be remembered that Mr. A would have been immoral just by willingly putting the girl in a position to get hurt, even if she never received a scratch. So also building nuclear arms (and other weapons that threaten the innocent), and aiming them at population centers in enemy territory, is immoral according to just war theory because it *threatens* to kill thousands, perhaps millions or tens or hundreds of millions, of innocent people. In effect, these innocent people are tied to the bumpers of nuclear warheads.

So-called limited nuclear weapons do not escape the logic of my argument for at least two reasons. First, their use would enhance even more than use of conventional weapons the possibility of "non-limited" nuclear weapons being fired. Second, it is by no means clear that use even of precisely targeted, "limited" nuclear weapons is of no danger to innocent people—such is the unpredictable nature of these weapons and their continuing efficacy after being fired, as George F. Kennan attests.[7]

Let me add to the three options listed in Chapter One, which were those logically possible if and when one accepts the prima facie legitimacy of pacifism within Christianity. (That is, first, one could reject one's Christianity, à la Nietzsche, because of its weaknesses; second, one could embrace pacifism as a necessary feature of Christianity; or, third, one could try to develop a theory within Christianity of a just war.) The following four options, or their variants, are those open if and when one accepts my thesis concerning the demise of the just war theory. I am claiming that if just war theory (the third option in Chapter One) turns out to be untenable, then the first two options in Chapter One should be looked at more closely and refined into the following four options:

1. One could return to the pacifism of Jesus and the early Christians, thereby opposing the construction of weapons dangerous to innocents from the start. I will return to the distinction between "nuclear pacifism" and full-fledged pacifism later, but here it should be noted that the defense policy of several of the great powers *centers* on nuclear weapons, and other weapons dangerous to innocents, such that opposition to these weapons is a de facto opposition to the defense establishments themselves in these countries.

2. One could cast one's country in the role of an Abraham killing (or threatening to kill) so many Isaacs. Because many, if not most, Christians who fight in war or who support their nation's military "know" that God is on their side, the popularity of this option should not be underestimated. The question of how these people know God's will, however, has no immediately apparent answer to someone like me, in that I have been waiting a lifetime to be struck off my horse. I am sure that my opponents will try to do so when they read this book, but that is not the sort of theophany I have in mind.

3. One could support the construction and/or use of nuclear weapons by some new theory meant to replace the just war theory. Unfortunately, the replacement often seems to be a crude form of utilitarian calculus, best exemplified by Harry Truman's defense of his use of atomic weapons: they saved American lives. If Christians take this route, it should be noted

that not only has the just war theory been buried but an entirely new direction has been set for Christian morality, a direction that conflicts with most of Christian morality's favorite doctrines dealing with the sanctity of human life.

This option, which I have previously called the necessary war theory (that is, war may not be just but it is necessary at times for survival), and which I will call the "war is hell" theory in Chapter Three, is especially slippery because its proponents often try to slip this wolf into discussions about war in the sheepish disguise of just war theory. I suspect that someone like George Weigel is in this camp, but I am not sure. He clearly says: "To my knowledge, no Catholic moralist is currently arguing that nuclear usage is tolerable under just war criteria, since nuclear weapons patently violate the classic principles of discrimination against noncombatants."[8] Well put, but Weigel obfuscates the issue when he commends the position that argues "with great sophistication for the unhappy but *necessary* ethical tolerance for nuclear deterrence" (my emphasis). We quickly learn what is beneath the veneer of this position when he holds that "the debate between pacifists and just war theorists is vital to the health of American Catholic thought today." Remembering what Weigel has previously said, we might ask, What just war theorists? A perplexing phoenix indeed.

4. Christians could admit that the construction of nuclear weapons is immoral, and then favor some form of gradual disarmament in order to extricate themselves from their moral predicament. For example, if I am choking a man I could immediately release him if it is brought to my attention that I am acting immorally. But if I am holding him hostage in a room whose only door is rigged with a bomb, upon realizing that I had acted immorally I would have to continue to hold him hostage for a while, until I could make it safe for him to leave. To paraphrase Iris Murdoch: Better Christians never would have

gotten into this nuclear predicament in the first place, but given this predicament, Christians could do no better than to gradually disarm.

Even this fourth option is bothersome to pacifists, as we will see in the Epilogue, but it is nonetheless more tolerable than options 2 and 3. And it must be admitted that those who hold this fourth option should not be confused with those who favor disarmament but who do not see anything intrinsically immoral in the construction of nuclear weapons (for example, George F. Kennan). Some of these latter theorists are hard to distinguish from those who take the third option (like Weigel) by vainly trying to resuscitate the just war theory so as to include nuclear weapons and other weapons that are designed to threaten or kill innocents. Because of the aforementioned logic of nuclear weapons in the light of just war prohibitions, they might have better luck trying to bring back the dinosaurs.

Death often goes unnoticed. Geocentrism lived on for well over a century after Copernicus; the theory of epicycles became a more and more cumbersome attempt to rescue a dead theory. We are witnessing the same sorts of effort today regarding the just war theory. In the Vatican II document *Gaudium et Spes* the destruction of entire cities is condemned on the grounds of the just war theory. Since this logically leaves open the possibility of destroying half a city, with innocents in it, one realizes that the church has implicitly, if not explicitly, given the just war theory its last rites. In the 1983 American Catholic bishops' pastoral letter on war and peace, threatening to use nuclear weapons is condemned, but making and possessing and aiming nuclear weapons is tolerated, as if these actions were not in themselves threatening.[9] Granted, the toleration of nuclear weapons is contingent on efforts to try to eliminate nuclear weapons (thereby approaching option 4 above), but the language used is more suggestive of option 3 in the sheepish guise of just war theory than pacifists could find acceptable.

Nonetheless, the bishops' letter serves the function of encouraging Christians to think about pacifism, at the very least.

Options 1 and 4 are both put under the label "pacifism" by some thinkers, making it imperative at a later point to clarify the differences among the sorts of Christian pacifism. (It will be seen that I am only willing to defend option 1.) Option 2, despite its popularity, is probably not worth much intellectual analysis because it is admittedly an unthinking position. It does, however, point out the difference between a crusade and a just war. The latter is justified on rational, human criteria, whereas the former is engaged in as a consequence of a divine command. Option 3 is in need of further analysis: does the supposed necessity of killing innocents in modern war completely forfeit any claim to morality in war? Obviously not, for *jus ad bellum* could be maintained even in the midst of atrocity. But as long as justice retains its meaning as rendering to *each* its due, *jus in bello* must have a place in considerations of war. If this just war theory still lives, and I only offer this suggestion to avoid the charge of dogmatism, it is a vicarious life engaged in only to supply the standpoint from which to clearly see its own inapplicability to modern warfare (hence the title of this chapter: "The *Pragmatic* Death of the Just War Theory").[10] And even technologically undeveloped peoples, through arms sales from technologically developed countries, fight in modern ways. If just war theory lives, it is only strong enough to sing its own swan song. There is really no reason, anyhow, to mourn the death of this theory. What is amazing is that it lasted as long as it did. Few theories have had as much success as this one in outliving Methuselah. May the just war theory rest, quite ironically, in peace.

The strength of my claim in this chapter can be seen if one compares it to the claims of the most sophisticated contemporary defender of the just war theory, James Turner Johnson.[11] Johnson astutely argues that a primary task of the Christian ethicist is to reintroduce acquaintance with what has been lost in Christian tradition.[12] However, as I see it, what has most tragically been lost is the pacifism of Jesus and the early church, as well as that of Saint Francis of Assisi, not to mention the loss of the just war theory's own absolute prohibition against knowingly killing the innocent. Johnson criticizes one popular view, which received scholarly formulation long ago by Alfred Vanderpol.[13] This is the view that suggests that it is always wrong to *intentionally* kill non-combatants, which, as we have seen, leaves open the possibility of killing some non-combatants if such killing is compatible with the proportionality dimension of the principle of double effect. But Johnson's critique of this view does not go far enough in that, in an analysis of Aquinas, he lists only three criteria that have to be met for a war to be just, all of them within the domain of *jus ad bellum:* right authority, just cause, and right intention. I hope my above treatment of Aquinas shows the inadequacy of Johnson's analysis.

In order to bolster contemporary just war theory it is to Johnson's advantage to suggest that the issue of non-combatant immunity was not explicitly treated in Aquinas and was only implicitly treated in his discussion of right intention, in that without the right intention in war one may *desire* to harm others, rather than only harm them reluctantly through a benign severity.[14] As evidence that *jus in bello* was only a "germinal idea" in Aquinas, Johnson implies that Aquinas's prohibition of churchmen from fighting was the most important *jus in bello* concern for him.[15] In short, if one is interested in non-combatant immunity "one must look elsewhere than to . . . Thomas Aquinas."[16] When Johnson does mention obliquely that "charity demands that the innocent be spared," it is by no means clear that he is referring to the position of Aquinas.[17]

Johnson has no objections to Aquinas still being cited as authoritative on war issues, but Aquinas's authority only lies in the region of *jus ad bellum*. Medieval principles regarding *jus in bello* derived neither from Aquinas nor from Augustine, but from non-intellectual sources: the chivalric code, custom, or *jus gentium*.[18] It is not that Johnson has some idiosyncratic conceptions of what discrimination of non-combatants from combatants or of proportionality are (or of what an innocent person is),[19] but he feels that because the chivalric code of non-combatant immunity was historically conditioned it no longer obtains in the same way it did in the Middle Ages.[20] The content of the chivalric (not Thomistic) code of non-combatant immunity "may easily appear out of step with contemporary reality";[21] hence it does not have the endurance of more formal philosophic principles. Therefore we should now be "more sensitive" to *jus ad bellum* and the start of wars, because once wars start new weapons and modes of war are more than a match for antiquated chivalry,[22] and hence, we are to assume, innocent people will be killed.

The evidence I cited earlier works against Johnson. Aquinas is clear that one may kill in war only those who *deserve* to be killed, that there is *no* justification for killing innocent people in war or for starving them or the like, and that the principle of double effect cannot be used to justify killing non-combatants but only the attacker (*invadentis*). What is odd is that Johnson develops his position while chastising Aquinas scholars like Vanderpol and Ramsey for telling us more about their own thought than that of Aquinas.[23] For example, Johnson is skeptical of the likelihood that Ramsey's notions (from which Ramsey himself sometimes veers) can be traced to Aquinas, specifically the notions of discrimination as an absolute guide and proportionality as only a relative guide to conduct in war. For Johnson, the earliest formulation of the notions of *jus ad bellum* and *jus in bello* together is in the sixteenth-century thinker Francisco Vitoria, and not before.[24] The use (or better, abuse) of Aquinas's comparatively minimal writings on war issues is analogous to the use (or abuse) Christians have made of the Bible for purposes of their own choosing.[25] From all of this one would expect that Johnson himself would be meticulous in his citation of Aquinas, carefully teasing out Aquinas's own words and phrases so as to avoid the apriorism he sees in other scholars. But this is not at all what Johnson does; hence I claim for eight additional reasons that his treatment of Aquinas is inadequate and that his effort to defend a contemporary version of just war theory is inadequate because he fails to preserve the best in the tradition of just war theory.

1. Although Johnson admits that for Aquinas there is a presumption against war, he does not emphasize the extent to which Aquinas is skeptical of the justness of war. Again, in Aquinas's key question on war in the *Summa Theologiae* (2a2ae, 40, 1) he asks, "Is it always (*semper*) a sin to wage war?" which seems to imply that normally, or on prima facie grounds, it *is* a sin to wage war. Or, at the very least, Aquinas implies that it is undeniable that sometimes it is a sin to wage war. The key question from the perspective of my book is whether the prima facie sinfulness of war is always due to *jus ad bellum* considerations.

2. Even if Johnson is correct that Aquinas's criteria for a just war are only three in number, and almost exclusively concerned with *jus ad bellum*, it is not the case that only right intention has implications for *jus in bello* issues. As before, just cause also has such implications. Aquinas defines just cause in such a way that "those who are attacked are attacked *because they deserve it* on account of some wrong they have done" (my emphasis; *requiritur causa justa: ut scilicet illi qui impugnantur propter aliquam culpam impugnationem mereantur*). If persons are attacked who are innocent of wrongdoing they have not been killed in a *just* war.

3. This is perhaps why Aquinas, relying on Augustine, exhorts us (2a2ae, 40, 1) to "be peaceful even while you are at

war" (*ergo bellando pacificus*). Not all actions in war are to be forbidden, but only those that are excessive (*sed inordinata*). Excessive response even in a war with *jus ad bellum* is to be prohibited.

4. Johnson fails to mention altogether the aforementioned passage where Aquinas commends (1a2ae, 105, 3) the law of moderation that should be adhered to in victorious wars, especially in the sparing of women, children, and food supplies (*instituit ut victoria moderate uterentur, parcendo mulieribus et parvulis, et etiam ligna fructifera regionis non inidendo*).

5. The only "exception" (1a2ae, 105, 3), as we have seen, to the law of moderation in war (that is, to *jus in bello*) is when we are ordered to kill innocents by God. Only when acting as executor of divine justice (*quasi divinae justitiae executorum mittebat*) can we kill non-combatants. Frederick Russell is surely correct that Aquinas's use of *deus ex machina* explanations diminishes the vigor of his prohibitions against killing innocents, but he is premature, along with Johnson, in claiming that it is difficult, if not impossible, to find a clear doctrine of non-combatant immunity in Aquinas.[26] As I see it, the cliché is helpful here in understanding Aquinas: *the* exception proves the rule. Or more precisely, a divine order to kill the innocent is not an exception to the rule, for in this instance (2a2ae, 64, 6) it is God who is responsible for the act, not God's human agent.[27]

6. What rule? it might be asked. The one Johnson and Russell completely ignore (2a2ae, 64, 6), a rule so fundamental it is worth repeating: "There is, therefore, simply no justification for taking the life of an innocent person" (*et ideo nullo modo licet occidere innocentum*). Aquinas could not possibly be clearer on this point. Yet just war theorists often speak as if Aquinas is only opposed to intending the death of non-combatants as an end and that he is not opposed to such deaths as a means. The bishops and the textbooks have ignored this

quotation as well, making it one of the best-kept secrets in Aquinas's thought. Because Aquinas believed that the cardinal virtue of justice referred to rendering to each its due, it is not unreasonable to speculate that it was because of a concern for justice that Aquinas was opposed to killing innocents, for the innocent person would never be receiving its due if killed in war. I know of no textual evidence whatsoever from Aquinas for the claim that "justice" "requires" us to do things we know result in civilian casualties. In any event, there is not sufficient evidence to conclude that Aquinas's position regarding non-combatants rests exclusively on non-intellectual sources, as Johnson alleges.

7. Although Johnson does not use the principle of double effect to permit the killing of some non-combatants (as do the American Catholic bishops and the Thomistic textbooks), he does fail to notice how Aquinas's use of this principle has the aforementioned implications for non-combatant immunity. A defensive act can have two effects for Aquinas (2a2ae, 64, 7): the saving of one's own life and the killing of the attacker. What is noteworthy is that Aquinas must use this famous principle to justify the killing of the attacker (*invadentis*); no other rational principles were left for Aquinas to justify the killing of innocents (only a divine command could do this). To speak colloquially, because of the fifth commandment, the pacifistic example set by Jesus, and so on, Aquinas was forced to "blow his wad" merely to explain how a Christian could kill an attacker. There is no indication that the principle of double effect could be used properly so as to permit the killing of even some non-combatants. The burden of proof is thus on the scholar who alleges that Aquinas would allow foreseen but unintended killing of innocents in war, and this burden has not yet been met by Johnson and other just war theorists.

8. Johnson and Russell[28] would probably claim that the passages treated in points 6 and 7 above do not deal with warfare

and hence are irrelevant to a consideration of non-combatant immunity in war. It must be admitted that 2a2ae, 64 deals primarily with homicide, but when Aquinas states that "somebody who uses more violence than is necessary to defend himself will be doing something wrong" (*et ideo si aliquis ad defendendum propriam vitam utatur majori violentia quam oportet, erit illicitum*), and when he favorably quotes the Decretals of Gregory to the effect that "it is legitimate to answer force with force provided it goes no further than due defense requires" (*vim vi repellere licet cum moderamine inculpatae tutelae*), he also makes it clear (contra Johnson and Russell) that these statements are exemplified by the soldier who fights against the enemy (*ut patet in milite pugnante contra hostes*).

It must be admitted that Aquinas is here (2a2ae, 64, 7) suggesting that, whereas a private person may not intend to kill another human being, public authorities may intend to do so. To be motivated by private passion when killing is a sin, he thinks, but not if one kills for the general good. But my position is not hurt by these admissions, because Aquinas's example here, once again, is the soldier who fights against the enemy (*contra hostes*). To say that public authorities or those acting for the common good can intentionally kill is *not* to deliver a carte blanche to kill innocents, nor even to permit the killing of a few innocents. Further, relying on Aristotle (*Physics* VIII, 4), Aquinas holds (2a2ae, 64, 8) that those who kill innocent people unknowingly—which is different from killing them unintentionally while trying to invoke the principle of double effect—must have previously tried to remove all possible occasions of homicide when they used violence, at least if they want to avoid guilt. With sadness we should note that in contemporary war it is not common to remove these occasions; indeed, because of the nature of contemporary weapons, such occasions are often actually welcomed.

In short, even the best contemporary defenders of the just

war theory have not been careful enough in their treatment of Aquinas, and it is lucky for them that they have not read Aquinas carefully regarding the status of innocents in war. In Chapter One I claimed that Aquinas's attempts to justify war were deficient. Here in Chapter Two I have claimed that, even if his attempts are sufficient to justify war, the stringency of his prohibitions against the killing of innocents, when considered along with the fact that the killing of innocent people has become a commonplace in contemporary war, should force the Thomist and the just war theorist to turn toward pacifism.

I would urge the same point on the American Catholic bishops. In their 1983 pastoral letter on war and peace they console the pacifist at several points. For example, they all but admit that Jesus was a pacifist (that is, Jesus's gift of peace was a life of non-violence), and they see the necessity of pacifism as a reminder to just war theorists that the ultimate goal of war is peace. In fact, it is hard to see why the bishops themselves should not adopt pacifism on their own criteria. They make it clear that "good ends (defending one's country, protecting freedom, etc.) cannot justify immoral means (the use of weapons which kill indiscriminately and threaten whole societies)."[29] There is a primacy to pacifism in that non-violent means of fending off aggression best reflect the life of Jesus.[30] This primacy affects just war theory in the insistence that no end can justify means that are evil in themselves.[31] To be precise: "No Christian can rightfully carry out orders or policies deliberately aimed at killing non-combatants."[32] Exactly. My argument in this chapter has been that this claim has fatal consequences for the just war theory.

No doubt the bishops were aware of the signs of these fatal consequences; hence they have taken drastic measures to save just war theory rather than adopt pacifism (with a few exceptions like Archbishop Raymond Hunthausen of Seattle). To suggest that the intentional killing of innocent non-combatants is always wrong seems to be a strong statement if we emphasize the word "always," but is a weak statement if we concentrate on "intentional" in that the bishops seem to permit foreseen but unintended deaths of at least some non-combatants. The bishops are aware that by condemning only "directly intended" attacks on non-combatants they leave the notion of intention in a vague state, because it is not at all clear how many deaths of non-combatants are "tolerable" as a result of indirect attacks.[33] On a single page the bishops illustrate the fundamental tension in their position: They suggest that "the use of any weapons which violate the principle of discrimination merits unequivocal condemnation," yet they equivocate by suggesting that a million innocent people killed "indirectly" or "unintentionally" is "perverted."[34] But what if fewer than a million are killed? When the bishops hold that "a narrow adherence exclusively to the principle of noncombatant immunity as a criterion for policy is an inadequate moral posture,"[35] we can see that the contradiction in their thought can only be resolved by moving to pacifism or war is hell theory.

The pragmatic death of the just war theory should not surprise anyone who is really familiar with the history of warfare. Donald Wells has done an admirable job in showing that there is now, and always has been in Western civilization, a conflict between what the laws of war prohibit and what is actually done in war.[36] Three military doctrines are responsible for the general failure to meet these prohibitions: military necessity, the supposed right of reprisal, and the military obligation of soldiers to obey superior orders. Wells examines in detail all three, especially the incredibly elastic doctrine of military necessity, which, with the rise of nationalism, now provides the guiding light in determining which actions will be performed and who will be killed in war.

The laws of war that have succumbed, "over the centuries," to the doctrine of military necessity come from at least four sources: the medieval just war theory; the jurists of the six-teenth to the eighteenth centuries, for example, Francisco Vitoria, Pierino Belli, Francisco Suarez, Hugo Grotius, and Samuel Pufendorf; the international congresses of the nine-teenth and twentieth centuries at Geneva, The Hague, the United Nations, and elsewhere; and military manuals con-structed by military officers themselves. (The last three were all derived from the sorts of principles developed in the just war theory.) All four sources have either been ignored or super-seded by other principles or by technological developments.

The history of prosecution of war criminals initially appears to be at odds with the contention that politicians and military officers have all but killed the notion of war crimes. We are convincingly shown by Wells, however, that the prosecution of war criminals has almost always been either half-hearted or, as in the case of the Nuremburg trials, exercises in the glorifi-cation of the victors. Also, because of the legal idiosyncracies of the Nuremburg trials, they can serve no precedent for the prosecution of future war criminals, as was evidenced in the war crimes trials (or lack thereof) arising out of Vietnam.

Nuclear weapons only represent the latest and most fright-ening example of weapons or military tactics that are designed to kill non-combatants or inflict unnecessary suffering, and hence of necessity lead to war crimes. Crossbows, the polluting of water supplies, cutting down or burning crops (as we have seen), lances with barbed tips, projectiles filled with glass, bul-lets dipped in poison, flame throwers, fragmentation bombs, and others have prepared the way for contemporary indiffer-ence on the part of politicians, military leaders, and, alas, citi-zens to war crimes.

A pacifist, however, must criticize Wells's response to the dismal history of war crimes. Although he consistently op-poses the war is hell theory, he wistfully hopes that changes in the "military-industrial-political" (I would add "educational") complex, and an increased desire on the part of the super-powers to heed the agreements made at the United Nations, will make war more moral than it has been in the past and war crimes less egregious. Why this fifth attempt to make war moral is supposed to fare better than the previous four attempts we are not told. Should Wells be so foolish as to enter where four shunned angels no longer tread? That is, Wells's thesis that there is now, and always has been in Western civilization, a conflict between what the laws of war prohibit and what is actually done in war lends more support to the pacifist option (which Wells largely ignores) than to the just war theory or, as he would call it, the position that opposes war crimes but can nonetheless allow or encourage war.

CHAPTER THREE

WHAT DOES

"WAR IS HELL"

MEAN?

THREE GENERAL POSITIONS are possible regarding the morality of war, quite apart from any religious orientation toward the world: the just war position, or something like it, which tries to determine *and apply* criteria for a moral war; pacifism, which argues either that war is not or cannot be moral, and hence one ought not to participate in it, or that war, if morally permissible, is nonetheless morally inferior to non-violent resistance as a means of responding to evil; and the position that holds that war and morality are mutually exclusive, so we should not be bothered by moral considerations when faced with war or the possibility of war. This last position has no common name, but appears under several rubrics: "necessary war theory," "military necessity," "realism," "*inter arma silent leges,"* "all's fair in love and war," "anything goes," "moral nihilism," "war is hell," and so on.

At the beginning of Chapter Two I suggested that for Christianity only two of these three options were available, in that the third seemed anathema to everything Christianity stood for. Even the just war theorists have admitted this. In fact, just war theory has more often found the doctrine of military necessity as its enemy than pacifism. But the times they are achanging. Recently the heirs of the just war theory have increasingly been speaking the language of military necessity and of the hellishness of war, as well they might, for if the just war theory has collapsed, one must, in order to avoid apathy, either go toward pacifism or toward the war is hell view. That is, quite apart from the arguments advanced in Chapter Two, defenders of modern defense systems themselves signal the pragmatic death of the just war theory by adopting the language and arguments of the war is hell theorist.

It is not surprising that philosophers and theologians have spent more time analyzing the just war theory and pacifism than the war is hell view, in that this last position suggests an absence of moral reasoning rather than the presence of it. The war is hell view is popular, at least by implication, but until recently it was only popular with non-philosophers and non-theologians. Two thinkers deserve credit for calling attention to the war is hell view—Michael Walzer and Richard Wasserstrom—but each could benefit from the other.[1] One aim of this chapter is to use these two authors together to show that the war is hell view is more complicated than many suspect, including these two authors taken individually. I will pursue this aim by analyzing the scope of the claim that war is hell as well as the claim's status. Another aim of this chapter is to pursue my method of logical exhaustion. There used to be two general views a Christian could take regarding war—pacifism in its different forms or the just war theory—but now that one of these views is between a rock and a hard place, its adherents have taken the protean disguise of war is hell theory, even if some still wistfully *say* they are just war theorists. But I will not be deterred; once the claim that war is hell is analyzed I will be one step closer to a positive treatment of the only theory left in principle for Christians to cling to when war is considered: pacifism.

I will use the just war theory as a heuristic device (which is compatible with its pragmatic death as a theory with which to act as Christians in the modern world) to understand the war is hell view. That is, looking at the war is hell view from the perspective of the just war theory *as if* the just war theory were alive and well may be profitable. Just war theory generally divided the moral reality of war into two parts, as has been seen: the morality *of* war and morality *in* war (*jus ad bellum* and *jus in bello*, respectively). The first distinction in the war is hell view that must be made deals with its scope. The more extreme variety rejects both *jus ad bellum* and *jus in bello*, usually because of some realm of necessity or duress, although this rejection often comes concomitantly in the form of talk about war in the language of strategy (entrapment, retreat, flanking maneuver, "backs to the wall," and all that) rather than in the language of morality. Karl von Clausewitz honestly argued for this view when claiming that war is never an activity constituted by its moral rules, and Thomas Hobbes implied it when he identified the necessity of war with nature. The Hobbesian version of the war is hell view lives on in metaphorical descriptions of war as a flood, as the grim reaper in uniform, or as "breaking out" like fire.

A less extreme variety of the war is hell view limits its scope to *jus in bello*. That is, one should have a just cause to fight in a war (for example, self-defense), but once the decision to fight has been made, anything goes. General William Tecumseh Sherman, who first announced that war is hell during the

American Civil War, seems to have held this version. He did not deny the possibility of moral judgment concerning war; in his view, war is entirely the moral responsibility of those who begin it, and no one can be blamed for anything done in defense that brings victory closer. A grey area appears, however, when this drive for victory is defended on the humanitarian grounds of saving lives, because then one may be—perhaps unwittingly—trying to introduce some type of just war theory. Utilitarian calculations in war are ambiguous: they may be morally neutral, but they can also be part of the just war theory or the war is hell view.

There are varying degrees of this less extreme form of the war is hell view. A sliding scale can be imagined where the liberties permitted in war increase with the strength of the claim to be fighting with just cause. If the supposed greatness of the justice of the cause takes away the inviolability of *all* moral rules in war (for example, those pertaining to innocents), then we end up at Sherman's end of the scale, killing babies and burning crops on the march through Georgia. Moving toward the opposite end of the sliding scale we end up . . . where? At the just war theory. But once we move away from strict observance of principles governing *jus in bello* we are in the war is hell view. There is no possibility of keeping to the just war theory *until* our backs are to the wall, then killing indiscriminately, and yet holding on to the just war theory. Taking one step toward the war is hell view is like contracting a deadly, incurable disease. There may be stages to the disease, but one either has the disease or not. So also, there are gradations on the scale of hellish war, but war is either hellish or not. That is, one either holds on firmly to the just war theory including its principles of *jus in bello* or one tumbles into the war is hell view. The difference between zero and a small number is finite, but when dealing with concepts of justice (that is, rendering to *each* its due) the metaphysical difference between being willing to kill no innocent people and being willing to kill some is infinite. Once one is willing to kill "only some" innocent people, how does one know when to turn back to justice? When the military necessity is over? And how does one know when the "necessity" is over? Are generals not notorious for claiming their backs are to the wall? Did not even Hitler claim military necessity in his conquests? And even if one did know when to go back to principles of justice once *jus in bello* was compromised, what would one return to? To one of the central principles of the just war theory that said, à la Aquinas, "There is, therefore, simply no justification for taking the life of an innocent person" (*Et ideo nullo modo licet occidere innocentum*)? And as Socrates is recorded as saying in Plato's *Crito*, who would find such an argument believable?

So much for the scope of the war is hell view. Equally important are distinctions regarding the status of claims made in this view. At least three sorts of claims could be made by saying "war is hell." The claim would be *descriptive* if it were a factual claim that issues relating to war are usually or always decided on grounds of national interest or expediency, rather than by an appeal to what is moral. The claim would be *prescriptive* if it asserted that issues concerning war ought to be decided by an appeal to national interest or expediency, rather than by an appeal to what is moral. Finally, the claim would be *analytic* if one were to suggest not that morality ought not to be considered when war is the issue, but rather that it cannot be considered. This last claim suggests that a moral point of view is meaningless concerning war either because war, by definition, is hell or because the actions of states are not amenable to moral analysis the way the actions of individuals are.

Walzer's fine treatment of the scope of the war is hell view and Wasserstrom's equally fine treatment of the status of claims in this view unfortunately do not interpenetrate in either of these two writers alone. If we put distinctions regard-

Diagram 1. War Is Hell

| | Scope | |
	Both Jus ad Bellum *and* Jus in Bello	Jus in Bello *Alone*
Status		
Descriptive	A	B
Prescriptive	C	D
Analytic	E	F

ing scope and status together, however, at least six possible positions within the war is hell view become evident (see Diagram 1).

The need for a diagram becomes apparent when one sees even a careful thinker like Walzer in confusion. At times he says that the war is hell view—he calls it "realism"—denies the meaningfulness of moral argument, implying that the realist's claim is analytic.[2] At other points he agrees with realism as a descriptive claim, because few wars in recorded history have adhered to the criteria of both *jus ad bellum* and *jus in bello*.[3] Perhaps this is why there have been at least some pacifists throughout the Christian centuries, but now that it seems impossible to fight a modern war with *jus in bello*, thereby indirectly affecting in some instances *jus ad bellum* (see the connection drawn between the two in Chapter Two), it is hoped that pacifism will regain its rightful place in Christian theory. At still other points Walzer denies the truth of realism as a descriptive claim in that war is the very opposite of hell, for in hell only those who deserve to suffer do so.[4] (Have the just war theorists who have defected to the camp of realism done well by this reflection?) Finally, Walzer disagrees with realism because it is *not* descriptive but a "doctrine," implying that realism is prescriptive.[5] Obviously what is needed is the awareness that "war is hell" can mean different things, and until these meanings are distinguished, Walzer-like confusion can be expected to continue and just war theorists can easily hide under the cover of realism.

Wasserstrom's stance, although not confused like Walzer's, nonetheless needs unity. His useful distinctions among the sorts of meanings the war is hell view—he calls it "moral nihilism"—can have[6] are unfortunately not used later when he analyzes the killing of innocents in war (that is, a *jus in bello* issue).[7] Thus, in effect, he gives the impression that the status of claims in, and the scope of, the war is hell view are unrelated.

How might the scheme developed in this chapter help in the defense of Christian pacifism? Simply put, it helps locate the directions in which the just war theorist might go when it is brought to light that just war theory is in serious trouble. The correct maneuver for the pacifist is to always bring the just war theorist back to the just war theory's own criteria and show their inapplicability in modern warfare, *and* to show the just war theorist how estranged the war is hell view is from anything remotely resembling an ethical approach to war. In that this latter claim needs support, I offer the following points: Defenders of C and D above (who defend the war is hell view prescriptively), because they rely on what we *ought* to do, are dangerously close to self-contradiction, because the war is hell view in all its forms, relative to scope, denies the relevance of moral "oughts" to war. What sort of "ought" is contained in C or D if not a moral "ought"? This remains unclear. Defenders of C and D should also be pressed to defend the basis upon which their incredibly far-reaching claims are made. Further, the defenders of D but not C (for example, General Sherman and fallen-away just war theorists) should be asked how the moral concerns that are so important when establishing the justice of a war's cause can be so easily set aside once a war starts. How much of a basketball must one cut away before one no longer has a basketball? Far less than half, or else "it" would no longer hold air and hence "it" would not be a basketball. Now take away *jus in bello* and how much justice is left in war? Some would say whatever is found in the *jus ad bellum* half, but half of what?

Positions A and B, which defend war is hell theory descriptively, are prone to a somewhat related sort of inconsistency, as Walzer has ably shown. To describe war without moral terms (aggression, self-defense, cruelty, appeasement, ruthlessness, atrocity, massacre, and so on) would be a difficult, if not impossible, task; yet this is what defenders of A and B would have to do to develop a rationally acceptable theory, but have not done. It is a commonplace that hypocrisy is rife in wartime because generals and politicians perceive it to be especially important at such a time to appear to be moral. The hypocrite's presumption of moral judgments in time of war indicates, at the very least, that there are ways of describing war in moral terms (or better, in terms of immorality), only one wishes this were done more honestly. Further, the attempt to hold B but not A raises the question as to what phenomena are present in describing the justice of a war in general that vanish when describing the practices of war itself—and why such a vanishing? It is significant that the later Tolstoy, who was tempted by A or B, became a pacifist.

Wasserstrom's analysis of E or F—he does not clearly distinguish the two—points to the fact that these views are usually part of a more general effort to advance the claim that *all* moral language is meaningless. If this is the case, then some obvious objections to E and F would arise that are not my concern here. Also, Wasserstrom leads us to ask about the extent to which nationalism, not an analysis of moral language, erroneously leads some to believe that war, by definition, is hell. And the defenders of F but not E would have a particularly hard time, it seems, combatting the charge of arbitrariness. The scheme developed in this chapter is of help in that it makes apparent the fact that because of their family resemblance B, D, and F are all open to the charge of arbitrariness. In that B and D are the lairs of former Christian just war theorists, this fact should not go unnoticed.

The outcome of my method of logical exhaustion should now be clear. Christians historically have had two options to choose from regarding war. One of these options is no longer tenable; it has been made obsolete by our enhanced techno-logical powers of destruction. The only option that remains, however, is the one with prima facie reasons to support it on the evidence we have on the life of Jesus; so it is not merely the lesser of two evils that we must accept reluctantly. The attempt to avoid pacifism, once the untenability of the just war theory is discovered, leads not to some morally superior view "beyond justice," whatever that phrase might mean, but to some sort of confused intellectual defense of the barbarism in war that the just war theory was originally meant to counter-act. The choice now seems to be: pacifism in one of its forms or the war is hell view in one of its forms. But from what Christian point of view can there really be such a choice?

It should be noted that Walzer opposes both pacifism and war is hell theory. In his criticisms of pacifism, however, several legitimate claims are made. He makes it clear that pacifism, if it is to be rationally persuasive, must not be seen as the end of secular history, when the lion will lie down with the lamb.[8] That is, it must be seen not only as a moral position but also as a political one that can allow us to uphold the values of com-munal life without fighting and killing. It is not my aim in this book to defend the strengths of pacifism as a political strategy, but I do feel it is necessary to say a few words regarding its plau-sibility as a political strategy, a plausibility strengthened by the practical efforts of Gandhi and Martin Luther King, Jr., and by the theoretical efforts of Gene Sharp.[9] Further, we should not fail to notice, as an example of plausible political change, the non-violent "revolution" in Eastern Europe (except Romania) that took place at the end of the 1980s, a change thought impossible just a few months before. This revolution, as is well known, was spearheaded by Solidarity in Poland, many of whose leaders acted non-violently both for pragmatic and for principled reasons. That is, the monumental liberation of Eastern Europe came about (against all of the expectations of defenders of just war theory and war is hell theory) by non-violent means.

As Walzer notices, civilian-based defense concedes the overrunning of the country that is being attacked, but it calls upon the conquered people to make themselves ungovernable. Walzer does not consider the very real possibility that the reduction of international tension brought about by a pacifist government would make it less likely that it would be attacked in the first place. And Walzer is surely incorrect in claiming that a pacifist, civilian-based response to aggression "diminishes its [aggression's] criminality."[10]

Civilian-based defense would attempt to transform an aggressive war into a political struggle that, although it would have its sufferings, would be far less destructive than even a short war. The logistical problems of the invaders would be severe in that they could not (because of massive, non-violent, Gandhi-like resistance) even depend on local transportation or communication systems. Hence, their military élan might well fade.[11] As Walzer notes, one of the attractive features of this view is that it is *not* millennial. In fact, and quite paradoxically, the practicality of civilian-based defense is seen when it is noted that it has similarities to successful guerrilla warfare: both depend on patience and on a mobilized population that is prepared to act as a unit.[12]

Walzer illustrates well how, once one has criticized pacifism, one is inexorably drawn into war is hell theory. Indeed Walzer intends to resurrect just war theory after the damage done to it by the Vietnam war,[13] a resurrection inspired by what he thinks is the justness of the Allies in the second world war. But little by little Walzer fudges on just war principles until he ends in the war is hell camp. When one sees even a determined and reflective just war theorist like Walzer end up defending realism, one cannot help but think that it is imperative to get clear on the meaning of the claim that war is hell. Walzer initiates his move away from just war theory when he allows the justice of "throwing the first punch" in a war (chap. 5, "Anticipations"), as do Anscombe and Ramsey, as we have seen. Then he morally permits third and fourth party interventions in war, even if America's intervention in Southeast Asia is criticized (chap. 6, "Interventions").

The fundamental tension in Walzer's view consists in his Kantian criticism of the war is hell theory (and of the utilitarian theory of war in Henry Sidgwick), on the one hand, and his use of the principle of double effect to justify the killing of some innocents, on the other (chaps. 8 and 9, respectively). Wavering between these two tendencies, Walzer alternately condemns terrorism (chap. 12), yet permits some sieges and blockades (chap. 10), even though the latter two types of warfare can be the most deadly of tactics (for civilians) in conventional war.

"Asinine ethics" is a phrase that Walzer borrows to describe the (just war theorist's) effort to do justice even if the heavens fall (chap. 14). Walzer wants to defend just war theory *except* in conditions of "supreme emergency" when the laws of war must be overridden (chap. 16). His position is that "decent men and women, hard pressed in war, must sometimes do terrible things, and then they themselves have to look for some way to reaffirm the values they have overthrown. . . . We must look for people who are not good, and use them, and dishonor them." [14] He has Winston Churchill's use of Arthur Harris in mind, the dishonored scapegoat for Britain's bombing of German cities. (Note the vagueness of the phrase "for some way" in this quotation, and note Walzer's abandonment of Kantian morality in his choice of the word "use.")

The theoretical difference between the pacifist, on the one hand, and the Walzerite just war theorist-realist, on the other, is that the latter assumes, usually without argument, that there are some situations in which there is no moral course for a person to take, situations that force one (albeit reluctantly) to take the former alternative in the following Camus-like dilemma: We must be either executioners or victims. [15] The pacifist's response should be that although we often face problems in the moral life, we hardly ever, if ever, face di-lemmas (literally, only two roads). That is, reflective individuals know that non-violent resistance to evil provides a tertium quid between wanton violence and anaesthesia. Relying on Socrates, Kant, and (ironically) Saint Thomas Aquinas, the pacifist would insist on the catholic (and Catholic) principle that no one can ever really be forced to do evil, not even the lesser of two evils.

Before moving to a positive analysis of pacifism, I will take a respite from my defense of pacifism and speculate as to why the pacifist's position has not been met with a ready acceptance commensurate with its intellectual and religious strengths.

CHAPTER FOUR

A

PLATONIC

INTERLUDE

THE QUESTION TO which I would like to respond in this chapter is this: Why, given the pacifism of Jesus in the Gospels, do most Christians find it startling to hear the claim that Jesus was a pacifist? Not only do most contemporary Christians not believe that Jesus was a pacifist, they are usually taken aback by the very suggestion. A few preliminary answers come to mind. First, in that the word "pacifism" (although not its Latin root, *pax*) is relatively recent, it might be anachronistic to read pacifism back into the life of Jesus. But if the word is defined in a preliminary way, as before, as an opposition to violence as a means of settling disputes or as a means of responding to evil, there is nothing inappropriate in calling Jesus a pacifist. Second, many Christians equate "pacifism" with "passive-ism"; hence it might be better to talk of non-violent resistance to evil than to use the word "pacifism." And third, the cultural weight of the just war theory, at least fifteen hundred years old, has made pacifism seem to be less appropriate a Christian response to evil than the just war theory. And until recently the supposed ease of meeting the criteria of the just war theory, at least with respect to innocents, has lulled Christians into complacency.

But something more fundamental is at stake. When most Christians "see" Jesus in their mind's eye they do not imagine him a pacifist. Iris Murdoch, in her suggestive little book *The Fire and the Sun*,[1] attempts to defend a rather unpopular position: Plato's treatment of the artists. In this chapter I will try to support Murdoch in her defense; specifically, I will do so with two case studies of how Christian just war theory has received immeasurable support from the arts.

Murdoch is not uncritical of Plato; nor am I, especially regarding some of his views on war (cf. *Phaedo* 114B on forgiveness). Only one particular Platonic-based thesis will be defended here: Art may provide one of the highest obstacles in the pursuit of a Christian peace. To prove this conclusion my procedure will be as follows with respect to the first case study (the second case study will be briefly treated later in the chapter): First, I will summarize Murdoch's interpretation of Plato's thesis; second, I will study the various depictions of "Christ Cleansing the Temple" as they are exhibited throughout the history of painting; third, I will analyze the Gospel accounts of this event, showing how painting has prevented many from understanding these accounts; and then I will offer a rather controversial proposal. I hope my contraction of vision in this chapter is not myopic, but will bore an aperture through which we will be able to see Christian non-pacifists more clearly than ever.

For Murdoch, Plato emphasizes the height of the objective

of the philosopher (or, we could say, the theologian) and the difficulty of the ascent. The eternal forms (which are in *some* sense divine) are absent from us and hard to reach, but only these forms will satisfy the desire for truth and beauty. This fact is concealed by the consoling image-making of the artists, who blur the distinction between the presence and absence of reality. Art often ignores the journey to the forms and persuades us that we already understand the real.

Plato realized that there is a dangerous relationship between art and religion in that the former loves the area of ambiguity, preempting religion in that region. Perhaps this is one of the reasons why Plato wanted to keep the artists under such rigid control. Art instinctively materializes God and the religious life. This is most especially the case in Christianity. Because of their "historical" nature, Christian images tend to be taken "for real." The figures of the Trinity are so familiar to us through paintings that it almost seems as if the great painters are the final authorities on the matter, as the Homeric rhapsodes were in ancient Greek religion.

I ask the reader to engage in a simple thought experiment. Conjure up the image of the scene where Jesus drives the moneychangers from the temple. If I am not mistaken, this image will include a whip in the hand of Jesus, which is used to violently expel those who had defiled the temple. Tables turned over, coins rolling in all directions, and screaming animals complete the scenario. If I ask the reader to indicate where this image came from, I suspect that the reader would say that it had been seen somewhere before, either in a museum, or in an art book, or in a missal, church calendar, movie, or the like (which were most likely loosely modeled after paintings in museums).

I doubt if very many, if any, have had this image indelibly imprinted on their mind's eye because of an extended analysis of the biblical texts concerning this incident. Only another visual image could have caused the clarity with which we all "see" Jesus cleansing the temple.

The source of this visual image is not hard to find. It has a long artistic history, which is remarkable for both its clarity and its consistency. From the twelfth to the eighteenth centuries this event was painted by at least twelve major artists, all of whom agreed on the major details of the story.

The earliest depiction of the event that I have been able to find is a mosaic in Monreale from the late twelfth century.[2] Jesus, with whip in hand, is knocking over a table, causing havoc to the nearby animals, coins, and human beings. The stiffness and simplicity of the figures seemingly freeze the event for us, offering a slice of time that only a photograph could improve upon.

Giotto (13th–14th centuries) depicts a similar story in his fresco in the Arena Chapel in Padua.[3] The careening coins and falling scales are gone (probably because the patron of the chapel, Enrico Scrovegni, was the son of a notorious money-lender), but the frightened animals and human beings remain. It is obvious why they are frightened: Jesus strikes a pose that would scare even a heavyweight boxer.

Not even the wild imagination of Hieronymous Bosch (15th–16th centuries) could improve on this scene. His treatment of the event, now found in Glasgow, has Jesus and the money-changers on center stage, albeit a small stage.[4] Surrounding this centerpiece are whole towns, strange objects, weird poses and sins, an incongruous nativity scene (but no more incongruous than the prophet of *agape* and of turning the other cheek lashing others with a whip), and other Boschian commonplaces. But the whip and Jesus's violence remain as before.

The sixteenth century was the most popular of all for the cleansing event. Jacobo Bassano (16th century) paints the event in a moving way, whose only original feature is the presence of a woman receiving Jesus's whip.[5] El Greco (16th–17th centuries) painted the event more than any other artist. As with some of his other favorite topics (for example, Saint Francis of Assisi), his versions of this subject can be seen all over the world.[6] His early versions of this subject are typical of the man who chose them. El Greco lived in Venice during this period, and he must have been impressed with:

> the bustling life of the public squares of this mercantile city, where the merchants spread their wares so close to the church of St. Mark that their barrows scratched the marble and scraped the sculptures. Christ in his anger has seized the whip: "My house shall be called the house of prayer; but ye have made it a den of thieves."[7]

Later, when he moved to Rome and elsewhere, the busyness (and business) of this scene remains, as does the violent Jesus, who causes the twisted torsos to repel from his whip. The same violence can be seen in the oak panels of the event from the sixteenth-century Abbey of Jumieges in Normandy, now found in the Frick Collection in New York.

This feverish interest in the cleansing runs over into the seventeenth century, for example, in the work of Theodor Rombouts (16th–17th centuries), where Jesus not only uses his whip but looks down his nose at the moneychangers with a patronizing stare.[8] This is also true in the paintings done in the seventeenth century by one of the followers of Caravaggio and by Bernardo Cavallino.[9]

From an artistic point of view perhaps the best painting of the cleansing was done by Rembrandt (17th century): The figures are well balanced and finely emphasized, largely because Rembrandt abandoned the idea that this event had to be placed against the background of a monumental architectural facade. The cleansing event, for Rembrandt, is a human event.[10] Yet even he cannot refrain from depicting the event melodramatically. The painting has five characters: an angry Jesus in the act of whipping the other four. One would think that Jesus had his legion of angels with him, as the four to be whipped are all in terror. In fact, one of these figures shows the physical agony that Christian artists have usually reserved for those burning in hell. Who knows how Rembrandt would have painted this man *after* Jesus had struck him. Subsequent to Rembrandt the grandiose setting of this event (suitable for a Cecil B. DeMille movie) again came into favor, as is seen in the works of Luca Giordano (17th–18th centuries) and Jean Baptiste Jouvenet (17th–18th centuries).[11] *None* of the listings of this painting in the standard reference work, *World Painting Index*, offers us a portrayal of the event where Jesus is not violent to human beings.

Can the Jesus of the painters be compatible with the pacifistic Jesus described in Chapter One? That is, how could Jesus violently whip other human beings and yet claim that the greatest commandment for human beings is to love; that the love he had in mind was extreme in that it did not demand love in return; that instead of an eye for an eye we should turn the other cheek, even if the evildoer wants our possessions; that we should love evildoers even as they enact their injustices; that the meek and peacemakers are blessed; that all who live by the sword shall die by it; and that we should live up to these sayings even if it means our dying for them? Should we not be somewhat skeptical of the painters' "story," now firmly embedded in our imaginations, as telling us the truth about Jesus? If not, to put it frankly, Jesus did not practice what he preached and should not receive many of the accolades that he receives. However, a careful look at the Gospel accounts of the cleansing may help us out of this fly bottle.

The synoptic Gospels (Matt. 21:12–13; Mark 11:15–17; Luke 19:45–46) seem to point to one cleansing and John 2:13–17 to another, perhaps earlier, cleansing. But whereas tradition and artistic representation have it that Jesus violently removed the moneydealers out of the temple with a whip, the texts seem to suggest something different. The whip is not mentioned at all in Matthew, Mark, or Luke. This in itself is worthy of note, given the prevalence in art history, and then in popular imagination, of the violent cord. All that is asserted is that Jesus drove out all who were buying or selling things in the temple. We have no indication how he drove them out. Did he say "Get out" or did he yell vehemently "Get Out!"? Might not a "miracle man" scare off a crowd with mere words, especially when the traders probably already realized that they were in violation of the spirit, if not the letter, of the law? Or was it because of Jesus's upsetting of their tables and seats? But such speculation, although interesting, is idle. We are not told how he drove them out. What is important to note is that, first, he did drive them out and, second, there is no indication in the synoptic Gospels that he did so violently or even physically. Jesus may have done "violence" to several tables and chairs, but there is no evidence to suggest that he struck another human being. Perhaps this upsetting of objects would force one to define very precisely what is meant by the term "pacifism." If it is taken as an opposition to war or violence as a means of settling disputes or resisting evil, then perhaps one should add that this non-violence is with regard to human beings, not inanimate things.

What of John's description of the cleansing of the temple? Finally we come upon the infamous "whip." It was probably not a whip at all, but a lash made out of rushes (*phragellion ek schoinion*), of the sort still used to herd animals in parts of the Mideast today. But if Jesus hoped to drive the moneychangers out violently, why did he choose such an inadequate instrument? The answer to this question is again found in the text. There is no clear indication in John that Jesus drove out the moneychangers violently; in fact, there is no clear evidence in

John that he drove them out at all. The use of the word "all" (*pantas*) may well refer to the sheep and cattle (*kai poiesas phragellion ek schoinion pantas exebalen ek tou hierou ta te probata kai tous boas*). If he drove out the moneychangers at all, which is not clearly stated in John 2:13–17, there is certainly no clear indication that he did so violently or even physically. Perhaps, and again this is only idle speculation, it was the boldness with which Jesus drove out the animals in the first cleansing of the temple (described in John) that made the moneychangers fear him so—remembering his reputation as a miracle man and their own cognizance of their violation of at least the spirit of the law—when he cleansed the temple a second time (described in the synoptic Gospels). In this second incident, one can imagine, all that Jesus needed to do was say "Get out" to drive out the moneychangers. At any rate, Jesus's pacifism remains intact. What is really noteworthy in this incident is that Jesus's feisty pacifism did not preclude his actively resisting evil, nor does it preclude his use of irony or an acid tongue.

One can now see the danger art poses to Christian pacifism. The pacifism of Jesus, which is preserved even in the cleansing narratives, is distorted by the painters and *a fortiori* (because of the previously mentioned authority the painters have in a historical religion like Christianity) by those who try to advocate a Christian just war theory on the basis of Jesus's life. These theorists look for an opening in Jesus's life, however small, to climb through so as to reach just war theory. To close the opening, as I have tried to do, one must first confront over eight hundred years of artistic tradition. Returning to a Platonic image, we can say the following: Art often ignores the difficult spiritual journey that Christianity would seem to require (that is, the attempt to imitate the non-violence of Jesus), and persuades us that true reality is already here (that is, in so many guns, bombs, and other contemporary "whips").

The controversial proposal that I promised is this: rather than advocating the banishment of artists that Plato does (which conflicts with our contemporary attachment to civil liberties), why not *encourage* painters and art historians to study the less pretentious function of art found in the East, where, according to Murdoch, "art is seen as a humbler and more felicitously ambiguous handmaiden of religion."[12] In Islam one can find a "dignified puritanism" in the denigration of the portrayal of religious events and the encouragement of subtle geometrical works that, in true Platonic fashion, can just as well lead to meditation on the formal order of the divine. This need not lead to a dogmatic iconoclastic attitude, however. In Hinduism the magnificent portrayal of the deities develops a healthy mysteriousness that avoids the "terrible historical clarity of Christianity." And in Zen Buddhism it is "unpretentious very simple art" that is the best companion for the religious person. Plato would seem to agree, for he suggests (*Laws* 956B) that the transitory artifacts offered to the gods should be such as can be made in a single day. The elaborate paintings of the cleansing, however, for all their material beauty, have in their own subtle way been corrupting Christianity for centuries.

It may well be that aesthetic categories, broadly conceived, play a far more significant role in the opposition to Christian pacifism than rational arguments, which are scanty. Everyone is familiar with studies that suggest that violence on children's television has a deleterious effect on young people. Every nation has patriotic music that becomes especially popular in time of war, or preparation for war. The same is true of literature, and jingoism goes in and out of style in journalism. The visual media also have a long history of association with the military, as has been insinuated above, from statues of soldiers on horseback to modern recruitment commercials. Can even dance make us more warlike or peaceful? Plato thought so, as is evidenced in the remarks of the Athenian in the *Laws*. In the rest of this chapter I will analyze the relevant texts from this dialogue. That is, dance will constitute the second case study I promised above. Although my analysis does not deal specifically with Christian pacifism, as in the first case study, it will nonetheless bring to light the pervasiveness of the aesthetic threat to pacifism. Dance and violence, and the interpenetration between the two, may be just as much a feature of our world as Plato's, perhaps more so because of the integral place of dance in popular culture today.

Dance has its origin in the movements natural to all living things. In humankind, melody awakens rhythm, which generates a particularly human form of movement in dance, indicating an intimate connection between music and dance (673C–D). Dance differs from music in that the former has posture and gesticulation peculiar to it, while melody is peculiar to music (672C). It is with these distinctive features of human movement in dance that I am concerned.

Fine dancing as a whole (*emmeleias*) is of two kinds: the war dance (*pyrrichen*) and the dance of peace (*emmeleian*).[13] It is these dances that Plato concentrates on, but the fact that they are designated as "fine" (*kalon*) indicates that there are other, vulgar dances in popular culture that are outside his area of principal concern (*Laws* 816B–C). The pyrrhic war dance and the emmelia (dance of peace) themselves can have either a dignified or a ludicrous effect, ultimately making four sorts of dance (*Laws* 814E). It should also be noted that the word used to designate the dance of peace is a cognate of the word for fine dancing in general. The war dance seems to be the exception to the rule.

What features does the pyrrhic dance possess? It represents the valiant soul in battle and in the toils of enforced endurance, as in the depiction of the motions of eluding blows and shots of every kind by swerving, yielding ground, leaping from the ground, or crouching. The contrary depiction of motions of attack are also included: the shooting of arrows, the casting of darts, and the dealing of all kinds of blows. The variety and complexity of representational movements in the pyrrhic dance are supplemented by a plethora of abstractions, particularly those of a well-balanced posture and limbs kept straight and taut (*Laws* 815A). The emmelia dance, by way of contrast, bears on the continent soul of duly measured pleasure, where a graceful style becoming a law-abiding person and appropriate motions are of prime importance (*Laws* 814E, 815B).

The purpose of these dances, apart from the reverence paid to divine promptings that encourage dance (*Laws* 804B), is twofold: they help one to attain physical fitness, and they help promote mental excellence. Dance is not an elective in the education of youth, but a requirement, largely because it is one of the few bridges between physical and mental culture (*Laws* 795D). Physically dance leads to nobility and beauty of body, tension in limbs, as well as grace. In this regard dance is often hard to distinguish from either athletics, especially wrestling, or military training (*Laws* 673A, 795D, 814D).

But dance also aims to present works of poetical inspiration, with care for dignity and decorum (*Laws* 795E). It is here that the dangers of dance become apparent. Dance should conform to rational principles (*Republic* 412B) because it has such an intense effect on soul (*Laws* 791A). The pyrrhic dance by its nature predisposes one toward violence, and when misused can cause a dangerous frenzy. A proper pyrrhic dance, even when performed in full battle array (*Laws* 796B), is meant to prepare youth for gallantry in the field (*Laws* 942D). Anarchic violence is quite a different thing.

Plato was not a pacifist; he lived centuries before Jesus and over a millennium before technology's potions killed, for all practical purposes, the just war theory. Yet Plato aids the pacifist's case in two ways. First, he more than anyone else is responsible for preserving the Socratic dictum, which carries within itself the seeds of pacifism, as Martin Luther King, Jr., realized, that it is worse to do an injustice than to receive one. In that one cannot avoid doing, or threatening to do, injustice with modern weapons, Socrates' dictum is more applicable now than ever. Second, Plato is more aware than anyone else that apparently minute perception (*aisthesis*—hence aesthetic) can predispose us toward violence. Not even dance should escape our notice. Realizing this should make us acutely aware of the more obvious enticements to violence that we receive daily from the electronic media.

The emmelia dance can also, albeit indirectly, lead to a wanton violence. If dancers exceed the requirements of necessity (*Republic* 373B), or if one enjoys the frivolous nonsense of dancing girls at a dinner party (*Protagoras* 347D), then one will develop an anarchic temper antithetical to an intelligent use of *eros*. Unreflective, profligate emmelia dancing can lead, it seems, to unreflective, profligate violence. Or at least unreflective, profligate emmelia dancing leads to unreflective, profligate pyrrhic dancing, which can, in turn, lead to unreflective, profligate violence. A consideration of Plato would obviously be helpful when contemporary "slam dances," where some people have actually been killed, are considered. But this is the nadir. Not as severe are some types of disco dancing (as the lambada) or breakdancing or the violent dances in the endzones of NFL football games, which are only three expressions of the absence of Apollo in popular dance. Also consider the often violent movements on rock videos. A bit more complex would be a consideration of folk dances, which very often have patriotic overtones. Most complex of all would be a detailed Platonic analysis of various works of ballet, for example, "Spartacus" or the recently acclaimed "Murderer Hope of Women," which deal with issues relating to violence or war.

Apollo, not Dionysus, gave us rhythm, from which dance

arose. Hence he, along with the Muse, is or should be the patron of dance (*Laws* 654A and *Ion* 536A). The flailing movements of bodies drunk with a Dionysian spirit can only be avoided in dance if dancers learn to consecrate themselves in an Apollonian or Egyptian mode (*Laws* 799A). And if dance is taught with intelligence (*Laws* 813B), it must be done by teachers who offer dance students good models to imitate (*Laws* 798D–E, 809B).

Plato no doubt goes too far in defending traditional dances (*Laws* 802A) and in prohibiting innovations in dance (*Laws* 816C). But his point seems to be that endless, mindless innovation in dance fosters a dangerously unregulated taste (*Laws* 660B). He was no prude, in that he encouraged dancers of both sexes to see each other dance without dress, but within reason (*logou*) and good taste (*Laws* 771E–772A). Strange as it seems, the most glorious of all dances, that of the stars, provides the most noble of all models for human dancers (*Epinomis* 982E). Further evidence for Plato's open-mindedness regarding dance, despite the need to keep it within an Apollonian order, is found in his observation that the movements of the stars are too numerous to count (*Timaeus* 40C).

Because dance can have such a frenzied effect on soul—or cause serenity, as in emmelia dancing done to the flute—one can see why Plato takes dance so seriously. Our understanding (*gignoskomen*) of what is good and bad in dance, in particular the pyrrhic dance, with its incitement to violence, is a necessary condition for understanding what right education is (*Laws* 654D–E, 791A). In our world, where dance is often associated with violence, or at least with Dionysian passion and macho virtue, it might still be worthwhile to see Plato go through his paces. If even dance occludes our vision of peace, how much more likely is it that there are other blinders that prevent us from seeing what a bright light Jesus's pacifism really is?

CHAPTER FIVE

GANDHI,

SAINTHOOD,

AND NUCLEAR

WEAPONS

WITH MY USE of the method of logical exhaustion completed in Chapter Three, and with a consideration of the aesthetic obstacles to an appreciation of pacifism in Chapter Four, I am now in a position to positively state the case for Christian pacifism or, better, pacifisms. Because pacifism can mean different things, I want to examine the different meanings carefully to avoid confusion about exactly what I am defending in this book. I will introduce in an informal way a distinction between nuclear pacifism and other sorts of pacifism in this chapter, as well as a distinction between pacifism as a duty and pacifism as supererogatory. I will reserve for the next chapter a formal presentation of the different sorts of pacifism in all their array.

First, an exemplum, told to me by a colleague, of the time when Saint Francis of Assisi unsuccessfully pleaded with "Christian" leaders in the Fifth Crusade to stop the fighting. Not to be done in too easily, Francis then went to the Moslem camp to see if he could have better luck. Malik-al-Kamil, the Moslem leader, who reminds us of the Moslem man in *Khartoum* (Chapter One), was a rational person who saw the legitimacy of Francis's position, but he had met too many fierce "Christians" to heed the saint's appeal. The moral my colleague drew from this story was that pacifistic saints like Francis (or Gandhi or Jesus) may be right in theory, but the practical world just has little or no place for such saints.

In this chapter I would like to analyze the terms "saint" or "hero" as they are applied to pacifists in the nuclear age. I will use these roughly synonymous words in a purely moral sense with no religious implications regarding miracles or the like. In particular I would like to ask what it means to say that Gandhi was a moral hero or a saintly person. The reasons I have chosen Gandhi will become apparent in the chapter, as will his integral connection not just to pacifism but to Christian pacifism in particular. And eventually I would like to disagree with my unnamed colleague.

The best conceptual framework I know of that has been developed to deal with the matters at hand is J. O. Urmson's seminal philosophical article "Saints and Heroes." He notes:

> Moral philosophers tend to discriminate, explicitly or implicitly, three types of action from the point of view of moral worth. First, they recognize actions that are a duty, or obligatory, or that we ought to perform, treating these terms as approximately synonymous; second, they recognize actions that are right in so far as they are permissible from a moral standpoint and not ruled out by moral considerations, but that are not morally required of us . . . ;

third, they recognize actions that are wrong, that we ought not to do.[1]

Urmson rightly holds that this threefold classification is inadequate because it leaves out of consideration a certain class of actions performed in a heroic or saintly way. But not all heroic or saintly actions are outside this classification, as the following analysis of "saint" indicates. This should be kept in mind as we explore nuclear weapons from a moral point of view.

> A person may be called a saint (1) if he does his duty regularly in contexts in which inclination, desire, or self-interest would lead most people not to do it, and does so as a result of abnormal self-control . . . (2) if he does his duty in contexts in which inclination or self-interest would lead most men not to do it, not . . . by abnormal self-control, but without effort . . . (3) if he does actions that are far beyond the limits of his duty.[2]

That is, saint-1 and saint-2 achieve their heroic status merely by meeting their duty when others fail, and saint-3 achieves saintly status by going "above and beyond the call of duty." The actions of saint-3 are usually called supererogatory (*erogatio* is Latin for payment).[3] A preliminary example of a saintly action that is not supererogatory would be the case of a doctor who stayed by her patients in a plague-ridden city when all of her physician colleagues fled; and supererogation can be seen in the case of a doctor who volunteered to go to a plague-ridden city. If the first doctor were interviewed after the plague she might well say, "I only did my (Hippocratic) duty." But only a modesty so excessive as to appear false could make the second doctor say the same.[4]

Or again, a government official who swears never to give information to the enemy and remains silent even after torture by the enemy is a non-supererogatory hero. But Father Kolbe, a

Franciscan priest who asked the Nazis to kill him instead of a man with a family who was supposed to be killed, is a hero-3.

Although the actions of saint-3 (or hero-3) are saintly *par excellence*, we should not forget how hard the way of duty may be, and that doing one's duty can at times deserve to be called heroic or saintly. John Stuart Mill puts the matter a bit too commercially when he says that a duty can be exacted from persons as a debt because it is a minimum requirement for living together.[5] Yet Mill's intent is well taken by Urmson:

> While life in a world without its saints and heroes would be impoverished, it would only be poor and not necessarily brutish or short as when basic duties are neglected. If we are to exact basic duties like debts, and censure failure, such duties must be, in ordinary circumstances, within the capacity of the ordinary man.[6]

To take a parallel from law, Prohibition asked too much of the American people, and as citizens got used to breaking the law, a lowering of respect for the law in general followed.[7] So also, if we expect supererogation from moral agents (for example, if pacifism is in some ways supererogatory) then we might not only be disappointed, but we might also notice a general disregard for duties as well: "A line must be drawn between what we can expect and demand from others and what we can merely hope for and receive with gratitude when we get it."[8] It is significant that one of the things Urmson sees as a duty is the avoidance of inflicting violence on others.

Now to Gandhi, whose life's details are well known and need not be summarized here. All admire him as a moral hero or saint; he had his detractors, but never any enemies who were even remotely rational. But what sort of saint was he? Raghavan's Iyer's important book, *The Moral and Political Thought of Mahatma Gandhi*, is typical of the sort of confused response that one gets to this question. Albert Einstein is quoted as saying that future generations "will scarcely believe that such a one as this, ever in flesh and blood, walked upon the earth."[9] This implies that Gandhi's actions were supererogatory, transcending not only duty, but humanity as well. Such angelic hero-worship of Gandhi as a disembodied *cogito*, however, is a dangerous thing, as Gandhi's reading of Thomas Carlyle indicates.[10] In places Iyer seems to agree with Einstein, in that a hero "must be a monk, striving to become a saint," leading a life of *"continual* struggle" (my emphasis).[11] "It is obvious that the exacting vow of truth, tantamount to a vow of saintship, can be taken only by a few."[12]

This sort of sainthood is dangerous for two reasons: First, it exalts the individual and enables the individual to feel, as Iyer puts it, that "the world is his oyster" and that the supererogatory saint can denigrate others.[13] That is, going above and beyond the call of duty is often difficult to distinguish from failing to meet one's duty. Søren Kierkegaard's defense of a teleological suspension of the ethical notwithstanding, one wonders why Abraham is a holy figure (à la Aquinas; see Chapter Two), yet "Son of Sam," who also "heard" God tell him to kill, is not. Second, even if the hero-3 is heroic and not dangerous, the exalted saintly status "above and beyond" us means that saintly conduct does not necessarily have any implications for citizens or politicians who are mere mortals.[14] It is this danger that is exemplified in the attitude toward Francis of Assisi mentioned at the beginning of this chapter.

However, as Iyer at other places notices, Gandhi gives many indications that he was not this sort of saint. Even if he were supererogatory, there is nothing logically impossible in our emulating him, but the point I would like to make cuts deeper than this. Gandhi himself denied the title of saint (saint-3) or "Mahatma" (great soul), and not out of false pride.[15] He always felt that a true saint must be effective in society.[16] The hero in Indian legend, who provides the mythological backdrop for Gandhi's historical actions, used the potentialities that were dormant in all human beings.[17] As was so often true for Gandhi, ancient wisdom guided contemporary praxis. In a modern democracy all are potential heroes;[18] as Gandhi put it, "All cannot be leaders, but all can be bearers."[19] We must worship the contagious spirit of heroism, not heroes.[20]

All of this works against seeing Gandhi as supererogatory. His more philosophical concepts bear this conclusion out. A consideration of three of them will illustrate the point. Gandhi's most general category was *satya*, or truth, which consisted, among other things, in stating that which is the case in the realm of knowledge. The truth or validity of *satya* is mirrored in the domain of conduct by *dharma*: duty, moral obligation, or right conduct. It is interesting to notice that Gandhi often used his most famous notion, *ahimsa*, as an equivalent to *dharma*.[21] *Ahimsa* can be roughly translated as non-violence or the renunciation of the will to kill, but Gandhi saw it in positive terms.[22] Christian *agape* is not too different from Gandhi's intent. In fact, Gandhi's doubts about *ahimsa* when he left his native land were allayed when he read the later Tolstoy. If only Christians would notice the pacifism inherent in their own religion as easily as some Moslem and Hindu spectators. (This is why a consideration of Gandhi is quite appropriate in a defense of Christian pacifism.)

To practice *ahimsa* was not supererogatory for Gandhi, but reasonable. It is the "fundamental and perhaps the only way in which we can express our respect for the innate worth of any human being."[23] This claim obviously needs explanation, but in a preliminary way it should be noted that for Jesus, as well, to engage in *agape* was not supererogatory but a command (see, for example, Matt. 22:34–40). Both Francis and Gandhi would understand this.

It is quite difficult for us non-heroes to see the pacifism entailed in *ahimsa* (or *agape*) as obligatory. That is, not all those who use violence (*himsa*) seem to be violating a duty. But the cutting edge of concern for contemporary "Gandhians," found in nuclear arms, and other arms specifically designed to kill or to threaten to kill innocents, may vindicate the master's position. At least with respect to *these* weapons *ahimsa* is *dharma*. The *satya* of this claim can be established (see Chapter Two) on grounds far outside the pacifistic tradition: even the just war theory has condemned the killing of innocents. The admirable clarity of Aquinas is nonetheless haunting in its force: "There is, therefore, simply no justification for taking the life of an innocent person" (*Et ideo nullo modo licet occidere innocentum*).[24] This quote is worth continually repeating because those who try to keep the Christian just war theory alive would prefer this quote to remain one of the best-kept secrets in the history of ideas. Immanuel Kant would seem to agree with Aquinas:

> It follows that a war of extermination, in which the destruction of both parties and of all justice can result, would permit perpetual peace only in the vast burial ground of the human race. Therefore, such a war and *the use of all means* leading to it must be absolutely forbidden (my emphasis).[25]

Kant is one of those thinkers who held that eventually pacifism would have to be embraced by all moral agents. He would perhaps have been surprised to learn in the eighteenth century that the time for pacifism would come rather quickly. As long as one of the necessary conditions for justice is that each will receive its due, nuclear weapons, and others that at least threaten innocent persons, are unjust because their raison d'être is to kill or threaten to kill innocent people. Debates may arise with respect to the sufficient conditions for justice, but this necessary condition, as has been noted, is as old as the concept of justice itself.

None of this escaped the notice of Gandhi, who was killed in 1948, three years after the first use of nuclear weapons. In *Non-Violence in Peace and War*, Gandhi's few remarks on nuclear weapons have been preserved. His position is clear:

> So far as I can see, the atomic bomb has deadened the finest feeling that has sustained mankind for ages. There used to be the so-called laws of war which made it tolerable. Now we know the naked truth. War knows no law except that of might.[26]

> I regard the employment of the atom bomb for the wholesale destruction of men, women, and children as the most diabolical use of science.[27]

To hit the nail on the head: to be a pacifist in *all* situations *may* well be supererogatory, and Gandhi *may* well be a hero-3 in this regard. I will return to this issue in the next chapter. But to refuse to kill, or to threaten to kill, innocents is merely to meet the demands of justice, for if they are killed, or threatened to be killed, how can they possibly be receiving their due? In this regard Gandhi is one of those heroes who only meet their duty.

Gandhi anticipated those who would feel "justified" (as opposed to being just) in the deployment of nuclear weapons "because of Russians." He said:

> Let no one run away with the idea that I wish to put in a defense of Japanese misdeeds. . . . The difference was only one of degree. I assume that Japan's greed was more unworthy. But the greater unworthiness conferred no right on the less unworthy of destroying without mercy men, women, and children of Japan in a particular area. The moral to be legitimately drawn from the supreme tragedy of the bomb is that it will not be destroyed by counter-bombs even as

violence cannot be ended by counter-violence. Hatred can be overcome only by love. Counter-hatred only increases the surface as well as the depth of hatred.[28]

When Gandhi claims that what he has said is nothing new,[29] one wonders if he is referring to Jesus or Francis of Assisi. In any event, when conventional wisdom, political and religious leaders, and the various *éminences grises* of our educational institutions do not condemn outright nuclear weapons and such, but at most question whether we need so many of them, one realizes that what we need are many more nonsupererogatory heroes.

Was Gandhi's sainthood with respect to nuclear weapons sainthood-1 or sainthood-2? His almost lifelong non-violent struggle (*satyagraha*) against all forms of violence, including those that endangered innocents, included fasts, marches, jail sentences, and untold suffering. Certainly his meeting the demands of duty when others failed was done with great effort, but eventually the seeds of his stoic sainthood-1 bloomed into the halcyon solace of sainthood-2 (see Diagram 2). "Have nuclear weapons antiquated non-violence?" he was asked. "No," he replied. Rather: "It [*ahimsa*] is the only thing that the atom bomb cannot destroy. I did not move a muscle when I first heard that the atom bomb had wiped out Hiroshima. On the contrary, I said to myself, 'Unless now the world adopts non-violence, it will spell certain suicide for mankind.' "[30] And this truth needs to be repeated, he thought, as long as there are those who disbelieve it.[31] Gandhi's *practical* genius was to take the truth (*satya*) of pacifism (that is, the Kantian truth that human beings are dignified ends in themselves and ought not to be killed), a truth inspired by Tolstoy's *The Kingdom of God Is Within You*, and turn it into the truth-*force* of non-violent resistance to evil. His neologism for this practical, yet saintly, truth-force was *satyagraha* (see Diagram 2).

Diagram 2: Gandhi's Sainthood

Types of Moral Actions	Types of Heroism-Sainthood	Gandhi's Heroism-Sainthood	
Prohibited Acts			
Permissible Acts			
Duties	1. Performs duty with great effort when others fail 2. Performs duty without effort when others fail	*Ahisma* with respect to innocent persons (e.g., those killed or threatened)	*dharma* became less of a burden in the course of his life
Supereroga-tory Acts	3. Goes beyond duty	*Ahisma* in all instances?	

My defense of Christian *pacifism* is not meant to focus exclusively on *Christian* pacifism in that a healthy syncretism may help us to appreciate what there is to learn from Hindu, secular, or other pacifisms. The interpenetration among these has already been seen in that Gandhi's pacifism was (re)awakened because of Christian sources. Martin Luther King, Jr., in turn, helps us to better understand Gandhi and vice versa. Consider that in the *Republic* (501B) Plato holds that the philosopher (or, we could say, the theologian) must frequently glance in two directions: at ideal justice and at that justice that one can help to reproduce in *this* world. Philosophers have traditionally had trouble moving from the former to the latter glance; persons of action have traditionally neglected the former glance altogether. Gandhi and King were by no means great philosophers; nonetheless their enormous success at making our world a more just place—because of their visions of ideal justice—reminds us of Plato's description.

After an early struggle with Nietzsche, King became convinced of the power of Christian *agape* through a study of Gandhi.[32] King's syncretism helps us to realize that there is nothing myopic or sectarian about pacifism, even if Christianity is a most efficacious route to pacifist conclusions. King's method was to pick up conclusions from various thinkers who appealed to him, with each conclusion a tessera in the colorful mosaic of his own thought, which nonetheless maintained a consistent pattern. In fact, King's fascination with the notion that limited ideas in conflict yield absolute truth led him to call Hegel his favorite philosopher.

Likewise, he used Heraclitus to show that rumblings of social discontent represent not retrogression but the necessary pains that accompany the birth of harmony. King's methodological Hegelianism did not lead him to Marxism, however. Karl Marx could be used to reawaken Christianity to its social mission, but in ethics King always remained a Kantian, especially because Kant's respect for persons was believed by King to entail pacifism and had redemptive significance as a veiled condemnation of racism.

King's syncretism is especially evident in the sources for his belief that one has a moral obligation to resist evil peacefully, even if that means breaking the law: Socrates, Henry David Thoreau, Gandhi (of course), and (surprisingly) Saint Augustine and Saint Thomas Aquinas, the latter because of his distinction between eternal and merely natural law. It is also important to note, as I will suggest in Chapter Eight, that King the pacifist learned from Aristotle how not to think of God as an unmoved mover.

Now that I have admitted that a pacifist can be a syncretist, it is time to rigorously demarcate the types of Christian pacifism. Before moving to Chapter Six, however, I would like to note that Gandhi's and King's pacifism should obviously not be confused with the position of those who are in favor of nuclear disarmament, but who would retain "conventional" weapons. Douglas Lackey holds this view. He correctly notes that political "realism" or war is hell theory is the opposite of traditional philosophical realism in that the latter asserts the objective existence of abstract properties, including moral properties such as justice.[33] And he is correct that it is not only theoretical wisdom (*sophia*) but also practical wisdom (*phronesis*) that must bow before the rule of logical consistency.[34] Lackey also helps to keep the *Christian* pacifist honest by noting that the proposition "Small children should not be tortured to death" is more obviously true (indeed it is a truism fundamental to any moral theory) than the proposition "God exists."[35] But admitting this does not necessarily bother the Christian *pacifist*.

That is, Lackey helps the Christian pacifist to clarify the status of Jesus's prescriptions given in the Sermon on the Mount, prescriptions that, as we have seen in Chapter One, support the case for Christian pacifism. If they are interpreted merely as rules that one must obey in order to be a Christian, they do not necessarily have implications for non-Christians. But one of the purposes of this book is to indicate the rationality of Christian pacifism, or at least to indicate the parallel paths along which the Christian pacifist and the Socratic-Kantian moral theorist must now travel. Lackey emphasizes that it was Kant's genius to recognize that moral conduct is essentially exemplary, because morally proper action consists in choosing to act in such a way that one's conduct could serve as an example for all humanity.[36] And there is no way to universalize the killing of innocent people; there is no way that it can serve as an exemplar. We now must become blessed through peacemaking in spite of ourselves, in that there seems to be no way to make (supposedly just) war into a pedagogical model that we could be proud of.

Lackey correctly distinguishes between Augustine's version of just war theory and Aquinas's.[37] The former thought war could be justified, but not an individual right of self-defense; hence Lackey (somewhat misleadingly) calls Augustine's view private or limited pacifism. There seem to be several similarities between Augustine's and Lackey's views. When the concerns of others are threatened, if I understand Lackey correctly, one's right to be a pacifist looks more like a privilege.[38] What is somewhat odd is that Lackey himself points out that the supposed "good war" in the twentieth century (that is, World War II) was not fought by the Allies with altruistic motives.[39] It is not accurate to argue that the Allies fought World War II to save the Jews, nor that war was necessary to save six million Jews, since in fact the war did not save them. And it is not true that the war was fought to protect the freedom of those who were in the main areas of Axis domination—China and Russia—both because the Allies had little sympathy for people in these areas and because there was not a high level of freedom to protect in these areas before the war began.

Pacifists receive only small consolation when they read Lackey respond to the question "How many innocent people am I allowed to kill if their deaths are necessary for my own survival?" by saying "Not many" and that a nation's right to kill innocents is "not unlimited."[40] Such responses are so incredibly vague that they in effect give enough elbow room for the trigger-happy to enact any violence they wish, short of bombing cities or strafing whole villages. It must be admitted, however, that Lackey is aware of the fact that violence in war, sufficiently prolonged, perverts both winners and losers.[41] Gandhi and King would say that the perversion starts with the first death or, better, with the taking up of arms in the first place.

Lackey tries to preserve the strength of just war theory by saying that whatever is necessary in war is not automatically permissible, but what is permissible must, in fact, be necessary.[42] The problem here is with the word "necessary," a word that Lackey holds in check not by a condemnation of the killing of the innocent, but by the criterion of military proportionality, that is, by the claim that the amount of destruction permitted in pursuit of a military objective must be proportionate to the importance of the objective. But this (attempted) justification of killing the innocent can only be supported by a subjective criterion of "importance" that Lackey himself would otherwise seem to oppose, as in his criticisms of the subjective vagaries encouraged by the principle of double effect.[43]

As in the case of Walzer, what the pacifist wants from Lackey is consistency. He is correct that only some laws of war are based on convention (for example, that medical vehicles should display a red cross rather than a green one). If laws of war were merely conventional,[44] it would follow that unilateral violations of the law would not be the highest forms of wickedness. In fact, violations would then be easily justifiable if one were demonstrably fighting for a just cause, but then the laws of war would not really be *laws*.[45] That is, the view of *jus in bello* as conventional runs into pragmatic problems as well as those of consistency. It must be admitted, however, that Lackey does a more consistent job than Walzer in adhering to his own acceptance of the principle of discrimination between combatants and non-combatants, a principle that requires "that noncombatants should *never* be chosen targets of attack, *even if* considerably more good than evil could be produced by choosing civilian targets" (emphasis in the original).[46] But even Lackey is, at times, inconsistent.

It counts in Lackey's favor that he sometimes claims that it is never permissible to take civilians as targets,[47] and he is even in agreement with the pacifist's claim that it is more difficult than many suppose to justify the killing even of combatants. Consider his insightful (Gandhi-like) critique of the principle of double effect, a principle that, as we have seen, has been used in the (attempted) justification of killing either combatants or non-combatants:

> The distinction between *death as a means* and *death as a side effect* is fine indeed. Normally, we say that M is a "means" to goal G if, in normal conditions, the production of M guarantees the existence of G, that is, if M in normal conditions is a sufficient condition of G. But the side effect S produced in the course of getting G may be so closely connected with G that, in normal conditions, we can have S only if we also have G. This makes G a necessary condition for S, and S a sufficient condition for G! What, then, is the difference between a means and a side effect? [48]

(S can be a sufficient condition for G, for example, in acts of terrorism, strange as this sounds.) In interpreting this quotation it makes a difference whether S refers to killing an attacker as a side effect or to killing an innocent person as a side effect. From this analysis the pacifist would conclude not only that it is illegitimate to kill innocent civilians as a side effect of one's actions in war (Lackey usually agrees with the pacifist here), but also that it is illegitimate to kill an enemy soldier as a side effect of one's attempt to act justly. That is, there is no defensible logical distinction, as Aquinas and Lackey think, between killing the attacker as an indirect side effect and one's direct attempt to act justly in the world.[49]

One of the incentives to outlaw air warfare in the interwar period was the hope that such warfare would be a humane development in comparison to the trenches of World War I.[50] But obviously no one believes this any longer now that the lies regarding British targeting policy in World War II, for example, and American bombing in Cambodia have been exposed. Nonetheless Lackey is correct in pointing out that there was a grain of truth in the arguments of those who defended air warfare. It is hard to find a more tragic kind of warfare than the (conventional) siege or blockde, as in the British blockade of Germany at the end of World War I (where approxiately 800,000 people died) or the German siege of Leningrad in World War II (where approximately one million people died). Lackey's paradoxical response is *not* in terms of a defense of non-combatant immunity as an absolute principle, but rather in terms of a "better grounded" principle of proportionality.[51] That is, Lackey could, perhaps, tolerate some (how many?) victims of blockades or sieges. Is it the case, as Lackey alleges, that the "principal moral argument against torture is that the practice of torture requires morally twisted characters, persons who are hardly likely to confine their activities to the strict limits of military need"?[52] This is a utilitarian view that conflicts with the claim that the most important argument against torture is that the one being tortured is being treated unfairly. Both in Walzer and Lackey this utilitarian melody can be heard running counterpoint to their dominant tune. For example, Lackey implies that the real reason why French torture of Algerians or the Shah's torture of Iranians are bothersome is that these tortures played into the hands of revolutionaries.[53]

As before, a pacifistic follower of Gandhi or King would receive solace from much of what Lackey says regarding nuclear disarmament, but would be distressed to think that one of the reasons we should reduce nuclear weapons levels is to bolster conventional forces that, as Lackey admits, create massive destruction in their own right. Should we be worried that one of the reasons to reduce nuclear weapons is to avoid the *ineffec-*

tiveness of the Mayaguez incident, the Tehran rescue attempts, the Beirut barracks catastrophe, the Grenada invasion mix-ups, and the Stark debacle?[54] The pacifist is bothered not so much by the fact that these efforts were ineffective but that they were tried at all. Lackey is on stronger ground when he criticizes those who suggest that nuclear deterrence "works" from a moral point of view. Regarding the intention to use nuclear weapons if the other side uses them, Lackey correctly notes the following:

> The fact that it is unlikely that we will carry out the intention, and the fact that publicizing the intention reduces the chance that we will carry it out, are morally irrelevant. Suppose that I intend to strangle the next girl I see who is wearing a pink polka dot dress, and that I place an anonymous advertisement announcing my intention in the local newspaper. Pink polka dot dresses are rare, and my advertisement makes it even less likely that they will be worn. Nevertheless, it is immoral for me to make such a murderous commitment.[55]

The immorality of having nuclear weapons and the concomitant threat to use them is compounded when the possessors maintain a policy that they do not wish other nations to emulate,[56] hence running afoul of Kantian universality and of the importance in Christian-Greek moral theory of (saintly-heroic) modeling.

In the end it is unclear how Lackey can reconcile his admiration for a strong (conventional) defense, his wanting "the Army, Navy, Air Force, and Marines to be trained in the use of weapons that will win military objectives," with his admiration for pacifism and the civilian-based defense systems that have received serious attention in Sweden, Switzerland, and Yugoslavia.[57]

CHAPTER SIX

A

CLASSIFICATION

OF CHRISTIAN

PACIFISMS

I AM NOW FINALLY in a position to precisely classify the various sorts of Christian pacifism and to make clear which sorts I am defending. There are at least three types of pacifism that one could imagine, and three modes of approach that one could take to these three types. It might be objected that I have carefully classified the war is hell view in Chapter Three, and now I am classifying pacifism, but I have not paid sufficient attention to the nuanced differences among different versions of the just war theory. My reply is simple: there may well be different types of just war theory, but all of them, if the term "justice" is taken seriously, must have prohibitions against killing, or threatening to kill, innocents. By concentrating on this prohibition, and on the contemporary impossibility of its realization, I have largely eliminated the need to analyze the different sorts of just war theory, although my treatment above of the sliding scale whereby the need for *jus in bello* decreases as the strength of *jus ad bellum* increases indicates that I am not oblivious to different versions of just war theory.

I have already indicated why there are not sufficient grounds to prohibit pacifism (see Chapter One). The modes of approach to pacifism consist in either seeing it as permissible, or seeing it as a duty, or seeing it as supererogatory. The types of pacifism include, first, nuclear pacifism, where just war theory would be considered a live option *except* when nuclear weapons and other weapons that killed, or threatened to kill, innocents came into play; second, pacifism taken as an opposition to all war, even if innocents are not killed or threatened with death; and third, pacifism taken as an opposition to violence as a means of settling disputes, or as a means of responding to evil, in all instances involving human beings, whether in war or not. This third type is often called complete or total pacifism. When mode of approach and type of pacifism are considered together, nine options ensue (see Diagram 3). B, E, and H, which claim that pacifism is a duty, are stronger claims than the other six, with E being a stronger claim than B, in that E opposes all war rather than nuclear weapons only, and H being a stronger claim than either B or E, in that H consists in an opposition to all violence, whether in war or not.

I will analyze these options in order. My position on A, B, and C should be apparent already. Because of the arguments advanced in Chapter Two and elsewhere, my defense of B (which claims that opposition to the construction or threatened use of nuclear weapons is a duty) is obvious. Option A trivializes the issue, as if to say that it is a matter of indifference whether one kills with one's bare hands, a gun, or a nuclear weapon. To say that one is *allowed* to be a pacifist with respect to nuclear weapons and such, which is what A says, but one is not morally required to be a pacifist, is, in effect, to offer a defense (albeit

Diagram 3: Varieties of Pacifism

Types of Pacifism	Modes of Approach to Pacifism		
	Permissible	Duty	Supererogatory
Nuclear Pacifism	A	B	C
Pacifism as an Opposition to All War	D	E	F
Pacifism as an Opposition to All Violence Used Against Human Beings	G	H	I

a weak one) of nuclear weapons. But the inability to include considerations of justice in such a defense makes A untenable, even on the criteria of the just war theory. Option C also trivializes the issue, although not as much as A. To say that one is to be *commended* for being a pacifist with respect to nuclear weapons and such, as opposed to merely being permitted to be a nuclear pacifist, is some consolation to defenders of B. But only small consolation. C in effect ignores the intellectual rigor of B, as in Chapter Two, because C does not make nuclear pacifism a duty for individuals throughout a society but rather only makes it a commendable option. And to say that nuclear pacifism is above and beyond the call of duty leads one to wonder what one's duty *is*. Does it not consist in avoiding killing or threatening to kill innocents? Once again, C should be opposed even on the criteria of just war theory. That is, if just war theory were alive and well, pacifists and just war theorists would agree on a defense of B.

What, then, is the issue? At least two points come to mind. First, some just war theorists, as has been seen, try to escape B by attempting to justify the killing of *some* innocents. This is done either by a misuse of the principle of double effect, as I have shown, or by sliding, perhaps unwittingly, into war is hell theory. And, second, some just war theorists, or even some who call themselves pacifists, will treat B as a regulative ideal to be reached eventually, but not immediately, because of the danger of destabilizing missile levels too quickly. This view tries to make C a respectable position in the present, but in effect it makes nuclear pacifism largely irrelevant for mere mortals. For the sake of argument I perhaps should concede some legitimacy to this view, especially because, ironically enough, pacifists are often thought to be a bit too dogmatic in their proposals. The irony is that one could be called dogmatic for not being willing to kill another human being, especially an innocent human being, as if killing another human being was not the most tangible expression of dogmatic confidence. Hence I do not concede that C is a morally defensible position, although I am willing to admit that a version of C can be imagined that is better than most defenses of nuclear weapons, a version that is coupled with real efforts at disarmament—say, practically speaking, an immediate, unilateral, ten percent reduction in nuclear weapons levels to assure one's opponent that one was serious about eventually reaching B. (This version can better be described as unilateral initiative rather than unilateral disarmament.) If such supposedly extreme measures were not taken by defenders of C, then defenders of B could easily conclude that C was a ruse for the continued existence of the status quo, that is, the war is hell theory. When political and religious leaders have stated for decades that they are in favor of arms reductions, but then seldom do anything concretely to reduce arms—indeed at present there is only a lull in an arms *race*—then it is understandable why the defender of B would become cynical with respect to C's eventual solution to the moral predicament we are in.

Next, why would one take E (a position that suggests that we are duty bound to be opposed to all *war*) seriously? And how could one distinguish between E and H (which suggests that we are duty bound to be opposed to all *violence*) on some morally relevant criteria? Once again, weapons that kill or threaten to kill innocents are important to consider. There are those who would defend B but not E on the grounds that it is possible to fight a war without killing innocents. But what sort of possibility is this? There are no historical examples I know of where the United States, at least, has fought such a war in this century. In some wars (for example, Vietnam) the "rules" of engagement with the enemy could not help but kill or torture innocents.[1] In many instances soldiers were encouraged to kill innocents. (Think of defoliants specifically designed to starve civilian populations; napalm specifically designed to burn the skin off of, but not kill, those who are hit; dum-dum bullets meant to torture; the tiger cages; the "pacification" program where villagers suspected of harboring guerrillas were knowingly killed.) And even in the incredibly quick, supposedly clean campaign in Grenada, a mental hospital was bombed and over twenty people killed. Not surprisingly, the United States government tried to hide these facts.[2] That is, there may be some very abstract sense, perhaps applicable to less technologically developed tribes extant, in which it is still possible to use just war theory with respect to the criterion of discrimination as to who should be killed. But this is not a real possibility for America, or the Soviet Union, their allies, or those to whom they sell their advanced military hardware. This takes in a great deal of territory. Almost all the territory there is.

My remarks on E would be incomplete, however, unless I linked it with B. As long ago as 1950 George F. Kennan remarked:

The crucial question is: Are we to rely upon weapons of mass destruction as an integral and vitally important component of our military strength, which we would expect to employ deliberately, immediately, and unhesitatingly in the event that we become involved in a military conflict with the Soviet Union? Or are we to retain such weapons in our national arsenal only as a deterrent to the use of similar weapons against ourselves or our allies and as a possible means of retaliation in case they are used?[3]

Although Kennan is not a pacifist, he nonetheless favors the second alternative rather than the first. But the first strategy has unfortunately won out. See Kennan's words "integral" and "vitally important component." Our defense strategy *centers* on nuclear weapons. Any use of weapons by nations possessing either nuclear weapons or other weapons that kill or threaten innocents carries with it the implication that nuclear or other such weapons could be used if less powerful weapons fail. That is, opposition to E requires an absolute distinction between weapons that do not threaten or kill innocents, on the one hand, and those that do, on the other. Such a rigid distinction cannot be drawn any more because part of the efficacy of "safe" weapons is in their lying against the backdrop of "unsafe" ones. Like A, D (which merely sees opposition to war as permissible) is a weak view that leaves one of the key questions unanswered: can a nation with advanced technological means of destruction avoid either killing or threatening to kill innocents in war or, what is even more unlikely, use weapons that do not kill or threaten innocents in an efficacious way without indirectly relying on weapons that do kill or threaten innocents?

Both D and F imply that war can be waged by technologically advanced nations without killing or threatening innocents, and it can be waged without the support of defoliants, nuclear weapons, and the like as "enforcers." That is, D and F claim something that is either historically unsubstantiated or historically questionable, at the very least. The burden of proof at our stage of history is *not* on the person who assumes innocents will be killed when a war is started. Can just war theorists supply the burden of proof that is on them? Can they cite either historical evidence from our century or strategic evidence from our military planners that suggests that a just war, on the just war theorist's own criteria, could be waged? Perhaps the opponent to E should read the texts used in ROTC courses concerning the sorts of weapons students learn about, even at Catholic colleges, where war is hell theory is supposed to be anathema.

H is, admittedly, a difficult position to consistently adhere to; claiming to hold that all violence directed against human beings is immoral immediately opens one up to the charge of hypocrisy if mugged on the street, or if witness to a rape, where one might either fight or be tempted to fight. Yet the insistence of Jesus, emphasized in Chapter One, at the very least is enough for Christians to reject G, which merely suggests that opposition to all violence is permissible. The *issue* of complete pacifism cannot be a matter of indifference to Christians. The question is: must we adopt H, or is I (which sees opposition to all violence as supererogatory) acceptable? Running the risk of hypocrisy, not knowing how I would react when personally attacked, but hoping I would have the courage to turn the other cheek, let me try to defend H. As was noted before, *agape* is not an option or an elective for Jesus—which would play into the hands of I—but a command (*entole*—Matt. 22: 34–40). So also, Jesus orders us to "be perfect, as your father in heaven is perfect" (Matt. 5:48). What these passages point out is that in many approaches to morality outside of Christianity, the sphere of supererogatory acts is quite large at the expense of duty's sphere. Christians are commanded (that is, they are duty bound) to do things (feed the hungry, visit those in prison, and so on) that from other perspectives would clearly be going above and beyond the call of duty. H makes more demands on us than B or E. This is our cross to bear. Period. I have no clever remarks or spiritual insights as to how to bear this cross (integral to the life of Jesus, at least) with equanimity. Gandhi, Thomas Merton, Albert Schweitzer, Martin Luther King, Jr., Daniel and Phillip Berrigan, Dorothy Day, and the like do a far better job of this than I ever could.[4]

But clarity, I hope, is a virtue I possess to some degree. In this book I have supplied reasons, persuasive reasons I hope, in defense of B and E, and in rejection of A, D, and G. I think I have intimated how C, F, and I can be reluctantly tolerated, for the sake of argument, with a special tolerance for I, as long as these options are held temporarily (for example, for the reasons cited in the room rigged with the bomb example in Chapter Two) until pacifism is adopted at some time in the forseeable future.[5] But this reluctant tolerance of C, F, and I is not to be confused with the attempt to offer a theory that is morally defensible. The sophistry often associated with C and F in particular wears on the pacifist's sometimes extraordinary powers of toleration. I also defend H, but with the humility (it is to be hoped not the false pride) of one who has faltered in the past. To hold H one must say along with Augustine when he was thinking aright: "Late have I loved." The trick is to talk in terms of various degrees of difficulty in fulfilling one's moral duties without destroying the irrefragable demands of duty itself. In our culture it takes more heroism to consistently hold H than E, and still less to hold B, which, with the resurgence of pacifism within Christianity, is hardly a heroic position to hold any more. But even E and H are duties, at least if we take the law of *agape* as Jesus presents it (and E is now a duty on purely rational grounds, say of Kantian ethical theory). And if we do not take the law of *agape* as Jesus presents it as normative, there are at least rational arguments concerning the status of justice to support B and E. To hold even these two positions deserves the designation "pacifist."

Understanding the types and meanings of pacifism is enhanced by a consideration of the book by Jenny Teichman *Pacifism and the Just War*,[6] although, as we will see, Teichman wavers between a defense of pacifism and a defense of just war theory. She is correct that pacifism can refer either to a practice of non-violence or to a set of theories.[7] (She is interested in examining the latter.) But this theoretical distinction should not be seen as a real distinction in that consistent application of pacifist theory can result only in the practice of non-violence.

One of the reasons I would insist on the practice of view H is to avoid defending what Teichman oxymoronically calls "just war pacifism,"[8] that is, the view that suggests that war, in principle, could be just but it no longer can be just in practice. The more precise way I would put the matter is to say that the current impossibility of avoiding the killing of innocents in war should shake us out of our complacency to realize the severity of killing *any* human being. By considering the grotesque immorality of contemporary war we may come to realize the lesser immorality of previous wars in which deaths and mutilations of all kinds were inflicted; where injustice was involved on at least one side, if not both; and where the outcome was decided (by definition) in a test of might, a test that is inherently incapable of settling questions of right.[9]

The pacifist's case is strengthened by Teichman's distinction between structural (or quiet) violence and institutional violence.[10] The former consists in invidious inequalities of opportunity, income, education, or esteem—say, due to the results of historical racism or class conflict. The latter type of violence refers to the legally approved violence of the police or military. What is often ignored by just war theory and war is hell theory is that the very need for the latter is largely, if not exclusively, due to the former, as is evidenced in the historical and cultural differences among crime rates. That is, the pacifist's most far-reaching response to the issue of violent crime in the streets is to claim that the amelioration of quiet violence is a necessary condition for the amelioration of violent crime.[11]

Teichman's own view seems to be one of agreement with pacifisms B and E but not H, as can be seen in the following quotation:

> A dilemma: if the arrangements for seizing, trying, sentencing, and punishing criminals within the state are necessary, fair, and non-tyrannical; in short, if they are reasonably civilized and functionally separate, then they will be too unlike warfare to justify that activity. If, on the other hand, those arrangements are of the kind made in countries run by tyrants and gangsters—where incidentally it is often likely to be the case that just one single organization (the army) carries out all the functionally separate tasks of the criminal law which are listed above—then they are not themselves justified and so cannot provide justification for anything else.[12]

Police forces can be justified whereas armies cannot, on Teichman's view, because the existence of the latter often presupposes that all enemy combatants are guilty, a presupposition that becomes troublesome when it is realized that in warfare most of the time most of the active participants do not know exactly why their leaders have led them into war. On this reasoning, the only people who can count as guilty in war, unlike in street crime, are the ones who plan the war.[13] There is no necessity that the prosecuting forces fighting street crime will imprison or kill any of the criminal's relatives or friends. And punishment can take many forms, but war without death is logically impossible.[14]

The defender of H, however, could accept Teichman's tolerance for police forces only if one could receive assurance that when criminals were subdued not only that their relatives not be killed but also that the criminals themselves not be killed and that when incarcerated they be treated humanely with the possibility left open that they could be reconciled with the rest of society.[15] Once again, the practicality of non-violent arrest and incarceration of criminals, or of resistance to an attacker without maiming or killing the attacker, is not the overwhelming problem many make it out to be. As before, even in the worst possible case of a crazed gunman, the criminal can just as easily be hit with a sedative dart as a deadly bullet. And working seriously against quiet violence is, the pacifist thinks, the best possible way to prevent the existence of crazed gunmen in the first place.[16]

Just war theorists are prone to forget that, on the grounds of their own theory, the injustice of the enemy's war aim is a necessary but not sufficient condition of the justice of one's own war aim.[17] It is perhaps because these sufficient conditions for just war have seldom, if ever, been met that in the tenth and eleventh centuries soldiers had to perform penances for killing in battle.[18] The danger that the just war theorist faces is that when he notices that the achievement of the sufficient conditions of a just war is rare, he is left with the choice of either becoming a pacifist or becoming somewhat cynical. The extreme form of this cynicism is evidenced in war is hell theory, but even those just war theorists (like Vitoria in the sixteenth century) who see the killing of women and children as only relatively wrong are at least somewhat cynical about the moral life.[19] Confidence in the importance of the moral life entails the belief that one's own justice does not depend on what one's "enemy" is doing.[20]

Teichman's avoidance of cynicism is evidenced in the following quotation:

It seems that we will have to conclude, *pro tem*, that the thesis that the innocent must not be directly attacked in war, the thesis that a just war is possible, and the thesis that the distinction between guilt and innocence has an ordinary and straightforward application to those who engage in war form an inconsistent triad. Then which of the theses must be given up? To give up the first is to give up a central tenet of the just war theory, to give up the second is to give up the just war theory itself. Giving up the third leads, via arbitrary definitions, to intolerable theoretical quandaries.[21]

The word "directly," however, in the first sentence is bothersome, for it hints of an attempt to illegitimately use the principle of double effect; but if it is dropped this triad becomes even more inconsistent. The extreme cynicism implied in the willingness to kill innocents should not hide the less extreme cynicism implied in the commonly heard justification for killing combatants, that is, that combatants can be killed because they have "forfeited" their right to life.[22] But if this is true, then why should the just warrior worry about right intention? Why does one even need right intention when killing if the being to be killed no longer has a right to life, or a right to be treated with respect?

Teichman is convinced that there is a coherent concept of natural rights (especially the right to life), a concept that sees natural rights as inalienable (that is, non-transferable). A legal right can be transferred by sales, divorces, and so on, but not a natural right, because any being capable of holding the latter already has it.[23] Teichman (like Walzer) believes that some inalienable rights can be overridden, but not the right to life (contra Walzer). The right to life cannot be measured on a scale against the other natural rights because it is, in fact, the ground of all rights whatsoever.[24] The strength of this claim is evidenced practically when we talk about examples of violence or attack where people are killed. The just war theorist must redefine violence as wrongful violence or legitimate violence, and must redefine attack as wrongful attack or legitimate attack. But there is something oxymoronic, at the very least, in talking about legitimate violence or legitimate attack.

Whereas Walzer and Lackey start out as just war theorists and then slip into war is hell theory, Teichman seems to start out as a pacifist and then slips into just war theory. She indicates agreement with Hobbes's claim that one's right to resist those who assault you cannot be laid down.[25] I would put the issue a bit differently: one's right not to be killed and the obligation to refrain from killing sentient life are logically on a par and are, in fact, the same concept viewed from two different standpoints.[26] Although Teichman herself admits that she does not have an adequate argument in defense of Hobbes's view, she is nonetheless convinced that, although the right of self-preservation is only relative (in that it would not be legitimate to kill an innocent person who materially posed a threat without doing so voluntarily), the right of self-defense against an attacker is absolute. One wonders, however, if Teichman can thus renounce pacifism H and still consistently defend pacifisms B and E. Has she not let the camel's nose into the tent by defending the (Hobbesian) right to self-defense as an *absolute* right?

Neither the death nor the non-existence of a human being are necessarily evil. We do not mourn the time before our birth, nor do we need to mourn the death of a ninety-year-old who lived a full life. Once we realize that we are animals we should expect to die. But from this we do not have enough evidence to conclude that we do not have an absolute obligation to avoid killing human beings. That is, although death simply as such is not an evil, premature or ugly or painful death surely *is* an evil that takes away one of the most important intrinsic goods that a human being can have and the ground for other intrinsic goods: life. (Not all intrinsic goods are important, as in some minor aesthetic enjoyment that serves no instrumental purpose[27]—say, reading the batting averages in the Sunday paper.) Some seem to think that causing premature or ugly or painful death can be justified by saying that one chose the lesser of two evils, but this is not a justification but an excuse. By definition to say that one has chosen evil presupposes that there is something bad about one's actions that needs excusing.[28]

I am not convinced that there really is, as the saying has it, a damned if you do and damned if you do not situation regarding war. Consider these examples from Bernard Williams,[29] which have been used by philosophers to indicate that war does pose such a situation[30]—say, between wanting to avoid killing and wanting to defend one's country. Imagine a man on a runaway trolley who has to choose between steering it into the left-hand track (where it will kill x people) and steering it into the right-hand track (where it will kill y people). Teichman rightly argues that this is not a situation where the man must choose between evil deeds but "of choosing under constraint of circumstances between evil-outcomes. The trolley rider is *ex hypothesi* only marginally responsible (if at all) for those circumstances; the example, therefore, is not relevant to questions about obligations."[31] The pacifist insists that, regarding war, leaders in a state *are* in a position of responsibility in that they have time and ability to respond non-violently to potential enemies, time and ability that the man on the trolley does not have. Or imagine Agamemnon's supposedly forced choice between disobeying the gods and destroying his daughter. In some sense this is a conflict, but as Teichman suggests, this is not a conflict between real obligations but between what he took to be his obligations. As in the case of Abraham in the Old Testament, there is good reason for religious believers to suspect the claim that divinity calls one to kill one's child (or anyone's child). Finally, Anna Karenina's choice between her lover and her son is even less a choice between real obligations in that one commitment (to her son) is far more important than the other.

Teichman would agree that the burden of proof is on the person who would argue that at times we must do evil. On its face this is an odd, indeed a dangerous, position. But she sees the strongest argument against absolute obligation as lying in the possibility of a choice between performing an evil deed oneself and failing to prevent someone else from performing an evil deed.[32] Teichman leaves it unclear whether she rejects this argument. Because both pacifism and just war theory have come to Western civilization from Christianity,[33] there is a tendency to think that both of these views entail a belief in the absolute obligation to avoid evil. But because philosophical theories must, on Teichman's view, be consistent with "ordinary" moral codes, and because there is stronger—but not conclusive—evidence in favor of absolute obligation, Teichman does not quite hammer down the last nail into the coffin of the view that sees moral principles in war as only relative guidelines.[34]

In the end we are left with the following tension in Teichman's thought,[35] a tension that a consistent pacifism can eliminate: on the one hand, she says that it is not possible to decide between pacifism and just war theory because the latter may well be, in certain instances, the lesser of two evils; on the other hand, she says that the point is not to justify war but to abolish it, and only the pacifist exhibits a strong belief in *that*. Because the pacifist is the only one who, on the evidence of the pacifist's theories and actions, really believes that the point is to abolish war, Teichman's tension, I think, can be resolved by the pacifist. Further, as I have indicated above, there is good reason to be skeptical of the claim that one must, in certain circumstances, do evil.[36]

CHAPTER SEVEN

ON

FUTURE

WARS

Now that i have made clear which sorts of pacifism I am defending, I would like to explore what a Christian pacifist's attitude might be to future wars that could be fought. In the process I will make another suggestion about why war is so hard to remove from Christian consciousness, supplementing the suggestions made in Chapter Four.

World War I was naively called the "war to end all wars" by a generation that remembered the horrors of that conflict. But as early as 1932 the French philosopher and convert to Catholicism Henri Bergson noted in *The Two Sources of Morality and Religion* that "it is strange to see how soon the sufferings of war are forgotten in time of peace."[1] Not even twenty years after the war to end all wars had ended, the world was bracing itself for an even more cataclysmic fight.

No one dared to call the Vietnam war the "war to end all

wars." No one even thought of it as such unconsciously. Yet one cannot help but marvel, along with Bergson, at the ability of a culture to forget the suffering that had mesmerized it only a few years before. For example, less than ten years after the American withdrawal from Vietnam the United States had drawn up contingency plans for military intervention in the Mideast if oil supplies were threatened. As early as the week of July 1, 1979, the defense secretary for the Carter administration, Harold Brown, confirmed that the United States would commit its military forces to defending oil suppliers if "vital" United States interests were threatened. All of the major candidates in the 1980, 1984, and 1988 American presidential elections supported such plans. And these plans are still in effect as I write, especially because of continuing tensions between Iran and Iraq and between Israel and the Palestinian people as well as the tension between the West and various Arab states, especially Iraq. And the Mideast is only one spot among many in the world where another major war could start.

How is it that Christians can so easily acquiesce to plans for such wars? The continued fetish for just war theory on the part of Christians is partially to blame, as are the aesthetic underpinnings to our culture, as was suggested in Chapter Four, exemplified by films that glorify war or by "G.I. Joe" dolls and the like. But pessimists will suggest that this sort of situation is inevitable because of something more basic: the warlike nature of human beings. Other would agree with King Khaled of Saudi Arabia, who said in 1979 that United States intervention in the Mideast would be governed by the "laws of the jungle," which inexorably drive human beings and states to behave as they do.

If Christianity means anything, or adds anything, to discourse about war it must at least come in the form of strong opposition to this war is hell view. Bergson may give us some clues as to how pacifists should try to persuade others to pursue policies so as to avoid future wars. The war instinct, he notices, assuming that there is such an instinct, nonetheless hinges on rational motives. No war is a purely chaotic affair, even if the many historical examples of war illustrate that the rational motives connected with the war instinct have been extremely varied. Yet, for Bergson, we can get a simplified and stylized outline of modern conflicts if we imagine in our mind's eye nations as purely agricultural populations. In such nations people live off the fruit of the land, such that a subsistence level of crops is considered a blessing. As the yield of crops is increased through technological innovation, the population increases, an increase that is taken care of by industry, in that this surplus population become industrial workers and city (or suburban) dwellers. Because industrialization demands great amounts of raw materials for its manufactured goods, it will buy or trade for all the raw materials it needs from foreign countries.

For Bergson, the citizens may well become "internal emigrants," in that it is the foreign supplier that is their real employer, just as if they had actually settled in that foreign land. Now the crux comes when these countries (for any one of a number of reasons) cease to supply these raw materials (or threatens to close its canal, as in the case of Panama). The industrialized country considers itself condemned to starve to death, and it takes the only step it thinks it can in order to survive: It uses force. This means war.

Things never happen quite so simply, and Bergson realized this. But the plausible ring that this 1932 note has been given in recent years is worthy of consideration, especially by Christians and pacifists. For Bergson, the root of the difficulty lies in the industrialized nation's belief that it is in danger of starving to death. In reality, according to Bergson, people in such a nation consider "that life is not worth living if they cannot have comforts, pleasures, luxuries; the national industry is considered insufficient if it provides for a bare existence, if it does not provide affluence."[2] Thus, the cause of such a potential war seems to lie not with a human being's atavistic nature, but with extravagance (literally, with walking too far down a hedonistic road). One suspects that a nation like the United States, which spends billions of dollars on weight-reducing clinics, diets (even for its dogs), and low-calorie items ad infinitum is a far distance away from starving to death. The point is that when the leaders of a nation say there must be war to preserve liberty, one should make sure that they do not mean luxury.

It may well be that Bergson's attempt to reduce all modern wars to his model is too simplistic. There were wars before industrialization, which would seem to suggest that the causes of modern wars are more deeply rooted than Bergson would admit. In addition, as Kant maintained, international affairs may still be largely in a Hobbesian state of nature because there is no commonly respected authority to ensure peace.

Yet the power of Bergson's theory cannot be denied. In fact, like a fine wine it seems to be improving with age. Studies by anthropologists indicate that human aggression and warfare are not so much "instinctive" as they are functions of people settling in certain territories and developing a vested interest in those territories. There is indeed evidence that primitive peoples may have been less warlike than civilized peoples.[3] War is not necessarily a function of civilization as such, but it is enhanced by three variables often present in high degrees in civilized society: private property, frustrated personality, and egoistic morality. The goal of the pacifist, it would seem, would be to change the sort of civilization that fosters these phenomena, which in turn foster war. This goal should be especially compatible to the Christian pacifist. It is a commonplace in Christian rhetoric, yet paradoxically a still largely untested hypothesis of modern Christianity, that spiritual goods are more important than material ones. The three variables mentioned above are not hard to find in our "advanced" culture; and redefining "private property" as "materialism," and replacing "egoistic morality" with "finding one's place in the bureaucracy," makes them easy to find in socialist cultures as well.

With his theory as a guide, Bergson accurately anticipated the second world war as early as 1932, earlier perhaps than any other intellectual in Europe. This accuracy gives me the confidence to make my own Bergsonian, albeit hypothetical, suggestion: if we are to avoid a major war in the Mideast (we have already had several "minor" incidents there that have cost hundreds of lives, as in the raid on American barracks in Lebanon and in the American attack on the Iranian passenger flight) we must either hope for extraordinary good luck or drastically limit our supposed "dependence" on the petroleum that comes from that region. It is to be hoped that we can avoid the tragic conditions of Cassandra or Bergson: to have the ability to anticipate in at least a hypothetical way what the future will bring, but find no listeners.

It might be objected that other possible future wars could hardly fit Bergson's model, for example, a possible war in Latin America or with the Soviet Union. But is it not the case that, even in those Latin American countries where the United States does not directly depend on the natural resources of those countries, it indirectly depends on them to maintain "our" style of economics, such that if they "fell into the hands of the enemy" (socialism? Christians should perhaps (re)read Acts of the Apostles for examples of biblical socialism) our prestige would be hurt and eventually our control over market forces diminished? And has not Soviet leadership traditionally engaged in calculations at least somewhat analogous to those of American leaders regarding the people they have tyrannized?

But even if Bergson is all wet, which I doubt, what are we to think about future wars that could occur? The thought is, to say the least, frightening. Not only pacifists can take Arnold Toynbee's metaphor seriously: We may well be like the dinosaurs.[4] No doubt if they could have thought in a sophisticated way, the dinosaurs would have been puffed up with their own self-importance. No animals were as strong as they. But now dinosaurs are museum pieces, stuffed models, as we may some-day be on some distant planet. Receiving an imprimatur from the second world war, where even "the just" killed hundreds of thousands of innocent people, some have assumed that a major war in the future is not only survivable but also, in theory, possibly just. Not only could such a war never be just, but our monstrous anthropocentrism perhaps makes us, in our con-ceit, even more unlikely than the dinosaurs to survive on this planet.

Apocalyptic writings have been secularized in the last fifty years (a dubious inheritance from Christianity) largely as a re-sult of the cold war. But is it obvious that the Soviet Union is a threat to our security? There is a quite intelligible view of Russian history that suggests that in order for the Russians to save themselves from being conquered and forcibly assimilated by the West, they have repeatedly been constrained to make themselves masters of Western ideas.[5] This tour de force has been achieved at least twice: first by Peter the Great and then by the Bolsheviks, who borrowed a Western heresy. I say "*at least* twice" because of nuclear weapons, which provide a third desperate effort to partially Westernize so as to avoid complete domination by the West. And it should be clear that the West has posed a continual threat to Russia. It is ironic that Western fears of possible Soviet domination of the world have been felt with an absence of guilt for actually having dominated most of the world themselves. Great Britain, France, and others con-quered most of Africa and Asia, while the United States and some European powers carved up the Western hemisphere. Is it any wonder that the Russian psyche is paranoid? After major attacks by France under Napoleon and by Germany (twice in this century) in the most terrible wars in history, it is understandable, if not justifiable, why the Soviet Union has felt the need for a buffer zone in Eastern Europe to protect itself against the West. (As a Polish-American, I admit this reluctantly.)

My point here is obviously not to apologize for Soviet atrocities, but rather to suggest that ever since the fifteenth century, as Toynbee argues, the rest of the world has been forced to react to Western imperialism and to Western atrocities. Some non-Western peoples have opted for a Herod-like approach of obsequiousness to the West ("if you cannot beat them, join them"), while others have responded with a zealot-like antipathy to the West. Both approaches are understandable, as is a third option exemplified by Gandhi in India: non-violent resistance. The Soviet government, with the Russian people at its core, have brutally taken the second option. The question the pacifist must emphasize is: Has the West in the years since World War II done a good job of convincing Russia that it no longer poses a threat to Russian security? Hardly. Think of the childishness of Krushchev promising to bury the West and of Reagan predicting that there would be no place for socialism in the world in the twenty-first century. Appeasement is a weak position, consisting in making threats of violence against an enemy and then not following through on those threats. In order to avoid future wars it is important to note that pacifism consists in the moral strength exhibited in not taunting or threatening violence against one's "enemy," indeed in not viewing the party with whom one has a disagreement as an enemy in the first place.

Defenders of the just war or war is hell theories might object here that even if the Soviet Union has never attacked the West *yet*, it may well do so in the future, and this on the evidence of what has been until recently a history of totalitarian domestic policies. But there is little historical evidence of any strong connection between the justice or injustice of a state's domestic policies, on the one hand, and how it treats foreign states, on the other. For example, some democratic states treat both their own citizens and their neighbors well, while other democratic states have brutally established empires abroad while they treated their own citizens well (think of fifth-century-B.C. Athens in the Peloponnesian War or the French in Algeria and Vietnam). Likewise, some totalitarian states brutalize both their own citizens and their neighbors (as in Nazi Germany), while others pretty much leave their neighbors alone (as in Franco's Spain or as in China today).

Once again Toynbee is helpful:

> Since an early date in the fourteenth century, autocracy and centralization have been the dominant notes of all successive Russian regimes. This Muscovite Russian political tradition has perhaps always been as disagreeable for the Russians themselves as it has certainly been distasteful and alarming to their neighbors; but unfortunately the Russians have learnt to put up with it, partly perhaps out of sheer habit, but also, no doubt, because they have felt it to be a lesser evil than the alternative fate of being conquered by aggressive neighbors.[6]

Hence the aforementioned paranoia regarding a muscular Islam (a fear of which both goes back centuries and has affected recent policies in Afghanistan) and an even more muscular, Western variety of Christianity. It is to be hoped that liberalization of the Russian soul will occur soon, but it may take a long time because of the religious fervor with which the Russians hold their distrust of the West. The pacifist's task is to encourage a patient and conciliatory approach to this brutalized and hence brutalizing people. Having lost twenty-five *million* people in the second world war, the Russians in the

Soviet Union should be taken seriously when they plead that they really want peace.

Alfred North Whitehead encourages us[7] to look at religions not from any narrow time frame, but as moving gradually toward the realization of their ideals. He cites as an example the nineteen-hundred-year history of Christian efforts to destroy slavery before success was obtained, a success almost unimaginable in the Roman world into which Christianity was born. It is with a less than sanguine visage that the pacifist approaches the possibility of future wars. We are no closer now than over nineteen hundred years ago to eliminating war; in fact, we may be further away from success than the early Christians. And to take another two thousand years to gradually solve the problem of war, as we did slavery, may be a luxury we cannot afford. As well they might, in addition to assiduously working for peace, Christian pacifists must also look to God. In my last chapter I will try to sketch a philosophy of God appropriate for the Christian pacifist's positions. There is a practical imperative for pacifists to hope and work for success in this world, but there is also an intellectual imperative to think clearly about God and violence, especially in a world that may be doomed.

No one can really predict the future of war; hence I have kept all of my speculations hypothetical. But defenders of nuclear deterrence try to make such predictions by assuring us that nuclear weapons deter the opponent, and some cynics do so by predicting an all-out nuclear war within a certain finite amount of time. To predict the future with assurance or in minute detail is to take unrealized possibilities and act as if they were already made actual, like the past. Along with our plastic control over the future, our somewhat efficacious freedom, we must wait. Christian pacifists must not only learn how to act non-violently but also how to wait, which is a type of action that only makes sense, it seems, with God. Otherwise we wait for Godot.

This waiting, however, is not to be confused with quietism or inactivity. Both just war theory and pacifism have peace-*building* as their *telos*,[8] but the pacifist is increasingly skeptical as to whether the just war theorist takes this *telos* seriously. It is this skepticism that forces the pacifist to disagree with those who see pacifism on a smooth continuum with the just war theory and other views.[9] Nor is it true that pacifism is a product of just war theory, although it is understandable how some could say so[10] when pacifists like myself appear to "back into" pacifism by considering the defects in just war theory. This method of presenting my argument, however, should not allow us to forget that in Chapter One pacifism was seen to have a privileged status—logically and chronologically—within Christianity apart from the influence of just war theory. And as we have seen in Teichman and Peter Brock, Christian moral thinking on war has received various secularized versions, so that now such thinking represents Western culture more generally. Indeed, because of the rise of the West, Christian moral thinking on war has come to be a universal expression of the morality of war.[11] The plurality of ethical theories that are now used to defend pacifism and just war theory (utilitarianism, deontology, virtue-based ethics[12]) tends to hide the Christian roots of these positions.

Pacifists should not feel guilty about aggressively arguing for their case. The convenient (and nearly ubiquitous) distortion of just war theory that rules out only intentional killings of non-combatants[13] should be criticized whenever it occurs. The justification of nuclear deterrence on the grounds that it prevents nuclear war should also be vigorously analyzed and kept clean of the fallacy of false cause. If someone points out to an American wearing elephant repellent that such stuff is not needed because there are no elephants about, one should not rest content when one hears the response that the repellent is obviously working. "Just as we cannot conclude from the absence of elephants that the repellent has worked, we cannot conclude from the absence of war that nuclear deterrence has worked."[14] Nor should pacifists lie supine when just-war-theorists-turned-realists claim that there is, at present, a sharp break between morality and "prudence" and that we "must" choose the latter.[15]

Finally, there is no reason for pacifists to "get defensive" if their opponents allege, as they often do, that pacifism is just as other-worldly as vegetarianism (or mysticism). Although other pacifists may disagree with me on this point, and although I will only allude to my argument here,[16] it seems to me that pacifists should welcome the link to vegetarianism. If pacifists are opposed not only to killing or inflicting suffering on rational human beings (that is, on most human beings) but also to killing or inflicting suffering on non-rational yet sentient beings (for example, severely retarded or senile human beings *as well as* animals with central nervous systems), sentient beings who are, of necessity, innocent, then pacifists could learn from philosophical vegetarians and vice versa.[17] Francis of Assisi, Gandhi, Tolstoy, and others are helpful in noticing that the link between pacifism and philosophical vegetarianism is due to the reticulative desire to bring the varieties of non-violence together into a coherent whole. That is, to leave relations between human beings and animals, as well as between human beings and other human beings, in a fragmented state is to invite future violence to at least some set of sentient beings.

CHAPTER EIGHT

PACIFISM AND

PHILOSOPHY

OF RELIGION

ONE OF THE major complaints one could have with traditional Christian theism, which I will call classical theism (in philosophy and theology, as opposed to biblical theism), is that it either explicitly or implicitly identifies God as permanent and not changing. Saint Thomas Aquinas's unmoved mover is the most obvious example of this tendency, but in general classical theists (in Judaism, Christianity—Protestant, Catholic, and Orthodox thinkers alike—and Islam) see God as a timeless, supernatural being who does not change. In this chapter I will show why this view of God is inadequate from a pacifist point of view.

I agree with Stanley Hauerwas when he says that Christian pacifism is unintelligible apart from the theological convictions that support it. As I argued in Chapter Four, art has an important effect on how one will view Christian pacifism, but an even greater effect is produced by the abstract categories one uses (explicitly or implicitly) to talk about God. Hence in this chapter I will try to get clear on why an inadequate conception of God tends to play into the hands of the just war theorist (or war is hell theorist), whereas a more rationally defensible and consistent conception of God lends support to pacifism. In my discussion of the concept of God I will rely heavily on the thought of Charles Hartshorne, one of the greatest philosophers of religion in the twentieth century and a thinker who has thought through the connection between the concept of God and pacifism more carefully than any other philosopher.[1]

The term "God" can be said to refer to the supremely excellent or all-worshipful being. This definition closely resembles Saint Anselm's "that than which no greater can be conceived." But the ontological argument is not what is at stake here. Even if the argument fails, which I doubt, the preliminary definition of God as the supremely excellent being, the all-worshipful being, or the greatest conceivable being seems unobjectionable. To say that God can be defined in these ways still leaves open the possibility that God is even more excellent or worshipful than we can conceive. This allows us to avoid objections from Thomists, including the new breed of Thomists in analytic philosophy, who fear that by defining God we are limiting God to human thought or language. All I am suggesting is that when we think of God we must be thinking of a being who surpasses all others or we are not thinking of God. Even the atheist or agnostic would admit this much. When the atheist says, "There is no God," the atheist is denying that a supremely excellent, all-worshipful, greatest conceivable being exists.

The contrast excellent-inferior is the truly invidious contrast when applied to God. If to be invidious is to be injurious, then this contrast is the most invidious one of all when applied (both terms) to God because God is only excellent. God is inferior in no way. Period. To suggest that God is in some small way inferior to some other being is to no longer speak about God, but about some being that is not supremely excellent, all-worshipful, or the greatest conceivable. Classical theists often assume that all contrasts, or most of them, when applied to God are invidious.

Let me assume from now on that God exists. What attributes does God possess? Consider the following two columns of attributes in polar contrast to each other:

permanence	change
one	many
activity	passivity
necessity	contingency
self-sufficient	dependent
actual	potential
absolute	relative
abstract	concrete

Classical theism tends toward oversimplification. It is comparatively easy to say, "God is strong rather than weak, so in all relations God is eternally active, not passive." In each case the classical theist decides which member of the contrasting pair is good (on the left) then attributes it to God, while wholly denying the contrasting term (on the right). Hence, God is one, but not many; permanent, but not changing; and so on. Pacifists, as I will show, should object to this monopolar prejudice because many of the virtues associated with a peaceful life are unfairly discredited in the monopolarist's prejudicial assumptions.

Monopolarity is common to both classical theism and pantheism, with the major difference between the two being the fact that classical theism admits the reality of plurality, potentiality, and becoming as a secondary form of existence "outside" God (on the right), whereas in pantheism God includes all reality within itself. Common to both classical theism and pantheism is the belief that the above categorical contrasts are invidious. The dilemma these two positions face is that either the deity is only one constituent of the whole (classical theism) or else the allegedly inferior pole in each contrast (on the right) is illusory (pantheism).

Key in the production of monopolarity is the assumption that excellence is found by separating and purifying one pole (on the left) and denigrating the other (on the right). That this is not the case can be seen by analyzing some of the attributes on the right side. At least since Augustine classical theists have been convinced that God's eternity meant not that God endured through all time, but that God was outside of time altogether and did not, could not, be receptive to temporal change. Aquinas identified God as unmoved, following Aristotle, who was the greatest predecessor to classical theism. Yet both activity or passivity can be either good or bad. Good passivity is likely to be called sensitivity, responsiveness, adaptability, sympathy, and the like. Insufficiently subtle or defective passivity is called wooden inflexibility, mulish stubbornness, inadaptability, unresponsiveness (or, as we have seen Whitehead call it, anaesthesia), and the like. That is, opponents to pacifism err both by saying that pacifists are too "passive" and also by failing to examine carefully the positive features of passivity.

Passivity per se refers to the way in which an individual's activity takes account of, and renders itself appropriate to, the activities of others. Hence the pacifistic virtues associated with "passivity" are not opposed to a life of non-violent *resistance* to evil because passivity is really a type of activity, as in working hard to listen to the counterpoint in a difficult symphony, or in working hard to understand the strengths in an opponent's view. To deny God passivity altogether is to deny God those aspects of passivity that are excellences. Or again, to deny God the ability to change does avoid fickleness, but at the expense of the ability to lovingly react to the sufferings of others. These defects in the concept of God in classical theism are not unrelated to classical theism's easy acceptance of the use of violence.

It must be admitted that classical theists have always *said* that God is a loving God who exhibits preeminent sympathy for creatures, but classical theists have not made it clear how this God could also be a strictly permanent being who remained unmoved by creatures. Hence, God's strict permanence has tended to make classical theists deemphasize divine sympathy.

The terms on the left side have both good and bad aspects as well. Oneness can mean wholeness, but also it can mean monotony or triviality. Actuality can mean definiteness, but it can mean non-relatedness to others. What happens to divine love when God, according to Aquinas, is claimed to be *pure* actuality? God ends up loving the world, but is not intrinsically related to it, whatever sort of love that may be. Self-sufficiency can, at times, be selfishness.

The trick when thinking of God is to attribute to God all excellences (left *and* right sides) and not to attribute to God any inferiorities (right *and* left sides). In short, excellent-inferior or good-evil are invidious contrasts; but permanence-change, being-becoming, and so on are non-invidious contrasts. Within each pole of a non-invidious contrast (for example, permanence-change) there are invidious elements (inferior permanence or inferior change), but also non-invidious, good elements (excellent permanence or excellent change).

God is, in one aspect of the divine nature, lovingly related to the world; in fact, in this aspect God is the integral totality of ordinary causes and effects. But in another aspect, God's essence, God is conceivable in abstraction from contingent beings. It is only the latter aspect of God (the left side) that

Aquinas and the just war theorists came close to describing, yet they erred even here by making God into something of a tyrant, an Oriental despot, a God who was immune to influence by others. Dipolar theism not only distinguishes God from the "all"; it also makes God, in a way, include the "all."[2]

I am not talking about two gods, one unified and the other plural, and so on. (Notice that I can retain a stable identity throughout all the changes in my life; God does this in a preeminent fashion.) Rather, what are often thought to be contraries are really mutually interdependent correlatives, as Hartshorne emphasizes: "The good as we know it is unity-in-variety, or variety-in-unity; if the variety overbalances, we have chaos or discord; if the unity, we have monotony or triviality."[3] Supreme excellence, if it is truly supreme excellence, must somehow be able to integrate all the complexity there is in the world into itself as one spiritual whole. The word "must" indicates divine necessity, along with God's essence, which is to necessarily exist. And the word "complexity" indicates the contingency that affects God through creaturely decisions. But in the classical theistic view, traditionally connected in an intimate way with just war theory, God is solely identified with the stony immobility of the absolute. For a dipolar theist God's abstract nature, God's being, may in a way escape from the temporal flux, but a living God is related to the world of becoming, which entails divine becoming as well if the world in some way is internally related to God. The classical theist's alternative to this view suggests that all relationships to God are external to divinity, threatening not only God's love but also God's nobility. A dog's being behind a particular rock affects the dog in certain ways; thus this relation is an internal relation to the dog. But it does not affect the rock, whose relationship with the dog is external to the rock's nature. Does this not show the superiority of canine consciousness, which is aware of the rock, to rocklike existence, which is unaware of the dog? Is it not therefore peculiar that God has been described by most of the just war theorists solely in rocklike terms: unmoved, permanent, only having external relations, being not becoming?

The notion of a tyrannical God, albeit a supposedly benevolent one, cannot be logically defended, at least if this God is also one of love. Nor can such a God be defended through a consideration of the logic of perfection, where just war theorists have denied God those perfections on the right side, even if they have (inconsistently) attributed to God the perfection of love. But once God as tyrant was accepted by many Christians (that is, a God whom the world needed, but a God who could just as well do without us), it was easy for Christians to emulate this God and kill with a supposedly benign severity. Proud, willful, Christian militarists have played into the hands of atheists like Ludwig Feuerbach who claim that God is nothing more than the grandest anthropomorphism. Perhaps even more likely than the suggestion that human beings have emulated God as tyrant is the suggestion that unsympathetic human (or more precisely, male) power has been seen as a divine virtue.[4]

Some might object that only God possesses the degree of love that renders superfluous the non-sympathetic forms of power. But it is not hybris on the pacifist's part to at least try to rival the "power" of God's love. Because there is nothing cowardly in this type of emulation, the pacifist can agree with the just war theorist that there is something deficient in failing to veto the desires of a human tyrant, a failure that would lead to a net deficiency of desires for all. And the pacifist should realize that the attempt to veto the desires of a tyrant can lead to tragedy for both the pacifist *and* the just warrior.[5]

Although only God can entirely avoid specialization of sympathy without falling into utter superficiality, pacifists can have a more synoptic view of sympathy than can soldiers because soldiers have the almost impossible task of trying to sympathize with the people they kill. Militarists need to consider more carefully the perfection of divine sympathy; and pacifists need to be attentive to the energy of divine resistance to creaturely will at the point where its excesses threaten the destruction of creaturely vitality.

If love can be defined as the taking of the interests of others into one's own sphere of interest, then wars among human beings must make God suffer, for the greatest conceivable being would surely be affected by, or suffer with, those who suffer. Human discords will, through love, become discords within the Loving Being. Is this not symbolized poignantly by the cross? When classical theists–just war theorists (the two can, for my purposes, be safely linked) claim that God is good *because* God is active and not passive, are they not ignoring the possibility that the ultimate power, or at least the most admirable power, is that of sensitivity? This power is not a type of inertia or anaesthesia. As was previously suggested, God's passivity consists in how supreme activity takes account of, and renders itself appropriate to, the activities of others.

For all of the considerable strengths of medieval philosophers and Protestant reformers, very few of them noticed that the ultimate power is that of sensitivity; indeed most of these thinkers encouraged worship of abject physical coercion, "tinged with cowardice," as Hartshorne puts it.[6] However, there are direct and indirect uses of power. God acts on all things directly, but one person's purpose influences another person only by first modifying the other person's bodily parts. For this reason human power of sensitivity is indirect. But even more indirect than non-violent activity is the use of force defended by the just war theorist, a force that is indirect not only because it is mediated by bodily parts but also because it is used in a war that is supposed to be a means to ultimately achieve peace.

The root of the word "pacifism," as we have seen, is not

"passivity," but the Latin *pax* (peace). The difference between pacifism and inactivity can be illustrated in the lives of Jesus, Francis of Assisi, Gandhi, Martin Luther King, and others, but also in what most just war theorists would regard as the most difficult case of all for the pacifist: how to respond to Hitler. My aim in discussing Hitler is to refute the claims that pacifism is weak and flabby, that pacifism produces a deficiency of social awareness, and hence provides an untrue likeness of the divine life and love, and that the pacifist fails to face the tragedy of human existence.

At the end of his work *The Origins of the Second World War*, mentioned in Chapter One, A. J. P. Taylor makes the following crucial points regarding this war:

> Men will long debate whether this renewed war could have been averted by greater firmness or by greater conciliation; and no answer will be found to these hypothetical speculations. Maybe either would have succeeded, if consistently followed; the mixture of the two, practiced by the British government, was the most likely to fail.[7]

"Greater firmness" would have been Churchill's approach. But Chamberlain's approach, the one that failed, does not exhaust the possibilities. Appeasement is not the same as pacifism. The former is the "mixture" alluded to above, which in effect drew lines in the sand at Versailles and threatened Germany with retribution if it crossed those lines. And when Hitler crossed one line and nothing happened, then another. . . . But if pacifism is interpreted not only as an opposition to violence as a means of settling disputes but also as an opposition to threats of violence, a pacifist never would have been party to the treaty of Versailles in the first place. As Taylor suggests, pacifism or "greater conciliation" may have succeeded as well as "greater firmness."

Of course we will never know if pacifism would have succeeded against Hitler, but the point is that the just war theorist cannot claim to know that it would not have succeeded.
It seems unfair to blame the pacifist for the consequences of
the policies of Versailles. Violence (and threats of violence)
breeds. . . . An absence of these sorts of threats and a conciliatory economic policy (as John Maynard Keynes had suggested)
may have taken away the breeding ground for the Nazis and
Hitler. But even if Hitler would still have come to power, it
may still have been possible to nip him in the bud in the early
1930s or at any other time through Gandhi-like, non-violent
resistance from massive numbers of religious pacifists. The
various religious groups in Germany, however, failed to promote pacifism not because they were skeptical of its efficacy,
but rather because they were not necessarily opposed to Hitler.
In fact, as is well known, some religious leaders (who were
just war theorists, no doubt) greeted Hitler with open arms and
even made agreements with him.

In short, it has not been shown that pacifism could not have
worked either against or in Germany, nor that pacifism is a vain
attempt to rival God's love. On the contrary, the pacifist might
claim that both "greater firmness" and appeasement are consequences of a too feeble attempt at such mirroring. Pacifists are
well aware of the fact that we will die, a fact that is tragic if we
die too early or in a gruesome way, but they gain some small
solace in knowing that they will not kill. This solace makes
all the moral difference in the world, however. And pacifists
who are dipolar theists are aware of the fact that the tragedy of
our existence, when incorporated into the divine life through
love, makes God tragic too.

The superiority of pacifism to just war theory can be seen
when the concept of peace is examined in detail. As before,
pacifism has the advantage of being a more direct (and perhaps

a more powerful) exhibition of sensitivity to others than just war theory. Brute power is more indirect than non-violent resistance to evil because it kills to affirm life, it makes war to establish peace. The ideal of peace is not a detached, static, pure form with a life of its own, which is then imitated by human beings in the world. Peace enters into the real world only as a constituitive element in real becoming. Non-violence is a way of becoming—specifically, a more direct way of becoming like the Divine Becoming.[8] The way peace enters into the real world partially depends on the subjective approach of the person who brings it into the world. (In Whitehead's language, there can be diverse prehensions of the same eternal object.) Pacifism is perhaps only one way in which peace can be experienced, but the most appropriate way because of its directness and because of the great value-intensity in favor of peace that it yields. Brute power, as opposed to the "power" that comes from loving others and from acting as a model of love for others, is said by just war theorists to be, at times, although never when innocents are killed, an instance of sensitivity to others. But this can be the case only indirectly, and hence only remotely. As we have seen, pacifism is not strictly speaking "passive" in the perjorative sense of the term, but is a disciplined attempt to attain what we have seen Whitehead call "that Harmony of Harmonies which calms destructive turbulence and completes civilization."

The first step in this discipline must be the removal of acquisitive urges due to preoccupation with self. That is, the initial locus of peace is the individual, who is an example of and a contributor to peace on a larger scale. (But this is not equivalent to saying that the elimination of war must wait on the development of peace in each individual.) Acquisitiveness gets in the way of creativity because hoarding is opposed to advancing and preoccupation with self is repetitious, not creative. The selfish person prefers to travel along the already known and possessed paths of triviality. In a peculiar sort of way even this is violent: it is to choose to have the past dominate the future. The other subjective forms of apprehending peace include duty (where one feels obliged to be peaceful), compromise (where one is peaceful so as to attain something other than peace), or violence (where one coerces others for the sake of peace, as in the just war theory). Only a pacifist apprehends peace for its own sake, without a hybrid or bastardized apprehension mixed with militarism.

The direct, intense approach to peace offered by pacifism avoids the "temporary" (when will these "temporary" wars cease?) stopover on the way to peace provided by the arguments defended by just war theorists. God *is* love, we are told. And, as the pacifist commonplace has it, there is no way to peace because peace *is* the way. Violence consists in the determination of others through force. In place of a contrast yielding mutual satisfaction there is conflict, a vying for control rather than creativity. Non-violent actions alone preserve the desire to actualize the intrinsic value of every creature whom God loves. One of God's contributions to the world is to supply it with its initial aim, which is typified by persuasion rather than by coercion. Or as Whitehead puts it, "God's role is not the combat of productive force with productive force, of destructive force with destructive force; it lies in the patient operation of the overpowering rationality of his conceptual harmonization."

But once peace is apprehended, alas, it perishes; hence it needs to be apprehended often. Because acquisitiveness, preoccupation with self, and violence are all around us, the opportunities for such apprehensions are not hard to find. Yet pacifism does not have to be approached exclusively as a reaction against something. Whitehead reminds us that youthful minds of any age can think ideally:

At the heart of the nature of things there are always the dream of youth and the harvest of tragedy. The Adventure of the Universe starts with the dream and reaps tragic Beauty. This is the secret of the union of Zest with Peace: —That the suffering attains its end in a Harmony of Harmonies. The immediate experience of this Final Fact, with its union of Youth and Tragedy, is the sense of Peace. In this way the World receives its persuasion towards such perfections as are possible for its diverse individual occasions.[9]

And who does this persuading? God, of course, who not only persuades but, as the greatest conceivable being, *must* offer us the greatest model of peace. This is one of those profound passages that is perhaps best left on its own, but I cannot resist the temptation of emphasizing that "the sense of Peace" consists in an *immediate* experience. Mediation through brute power always keeps us at least one additional step away from peaceful becoming.

Dipolar theism (as in Hartshorne and Whitehead) points out the inadequacies in the conception of God as an active but not passive, unmoved (supposedly benevolent) tyrant. The God of the classical theists cannot be a God of peace, but only (quite ironically) an anaesthetically abstract God. This God cannot have dreams of youth, nor can such a God persuade the world toward "such perfections as are possible for its diverse individual occasions" because God does not persuade, but orders; much less can God be persuaded. (Persuasion presupposes a two-way street, as opposed to monodirectional, authoritarian dictation.) The conception of God as dipolar, a conception that can appropriate the best in the Gospels (as in a God of love), allows for a God who *can* do all of these things, and without mediation. Hence a pursuit of peace is a more fitting type of worship to give God than brute power.

As Kant foresaw, technological progress has made war increasingly destructive, and the rational ideal requires us to find other ways to deal with group conflicts. We need not fear God (a fear that makes sense if one views God as a monopolar tyrant) but ourselves and our fellows. *We* have built the foundations of hell on earth; hence we no longer need hell to frighten us.[10] In comparison to nuclear warfare talk of a supernatural hell "seems childish folly," according to Hartshorne: "Perhaps the threat of nuclear warfare, as close to absolute absurdity as one can fear to think of, will lead us to trust less to our individual and collective rages and greeds and more to our sympathies and admirations toward fellow creatures."[11] There is some small hope that there would be an end to the many centuries spent in worshipping (brute) power more than love (and being more than creative becoming). For example, a straightforward interpretation of God as eminent love was beyond Lincoln, who believed that the Civil War would last as long as God willed it to last. Like many theologians and philosophers, Lincoln was more willing to confess his "ignorance of God's goodness than of his power."

No book can answer all questions. Mine will not satisfy those (like Anscombe et al.) who want a God to be feared, nor can I claim allegiance to the brutal God often described in the Old Testament, rearing its ugly head again in the last book of the New Testament. As I see it, this being not only is not the all-worshipful being but is actually morally inferior to many human beings I have met, as Carl Jung has also pointed out.[12] I hope I have made at least some progress, however, in showing that Christian pacifism is not dependent on syrupy sentimentalism. If acerbic at times, I would nonetheless like to think of my arguments as attempts at rational persuasion. Small progress is all I have hoped for here (even if slow steps forward may not be sufficient to save our species on this planet), because when dealing with issues too deep for tears, as Wordsworth put it—God and peace—getting a little closer to the truth may be going a long way.

Perhaps it will be objected that my treatment of the relationship between God as dipolar and pacifism is somewhat simpleminded in that institutional responsibilities can only be conceived of as complex because there are various kinds and levels of duty. For example, Whitehead himself was not a pacifist because, according to Paul Kuntz,[13] he thought it best to serve God *through* church and state and university; hence the goal was to balance one's institutional duties so as to find a sequence in which all duties could be fulfilled. But such a balancing seems muddleheaded, to paraphrase Bertrand Russell. Exactly *how* can one fulfill one's "duty" to the state in war by killing, or by being prepared to kill, innocent people while simultaneously (or subsequently?) fulfilling one's religious and philosophical duty not to kill innocent people? That is, paradoxically (because Russell was not a theist) there is something that the theist can learn from Russell's "simplemindedness" as opposed to Whitehead's "muddleheadedness."

The pacifist—whether an agnostic like Russell or a theist—recognizes only a few duties, but these are enough to make sense of the moral life; indeed they are the only principles by which one can make sense of the moral life. The prohibition against killing human beings, especially innocent human beings, is one of these duties, such that "balancing" this duty against patriotic urges cannot help but create a moral muddle. Kuntz is correct that one of the tragedies of our age is that ideological differences between, say, Whitehead's national loyalty in World War I and Russell's pacifism cannot be held together by a philosophic center. Just war theory once claimed to be a tertium quid between militarism, on the one hand, and pacifism, on the other. But, as I have alleged throughout this book, any careful observer of twentieth-century warfare will notice that just war theory has turned out to be a bogus center. As

Arthur Miller indicates in his play *The Crucible*, there are certain issues that, when melted in a moral crucible, separate out into two and only two options.

I am well aware of the fact that there will continue to be efforts to provide just war theory a central role. For example, Sidney Axinn has argued that one can still act in a dignified way under battlefield conditions as long as one obeys the laws of war found in the Hague and Geneva conventions,[14] but these are conventions that, as I have noted, even the "just side" in the two world wars and other conflicts have repeatedly flaunted and then disobeyed. Duane Cady's view is much closer to the truth, I think, especially when he claims that morality entails a move (albeit a reluctant one, in Cady's case) from "warism" to pacifism. However, he weakens whatever distinctiveness pacifism may have by placing it on a continuum with "warism" rather than as a discrete position in its own right, a position that can only be reached by a quantum jump away from violence as a means of settling disputes.[15]

Closer still to the truth, I think, is the view of Robert Holmes,[16] who collapses both just war theory and war is hell theory into "militarism." That is, the majority of people, who live friendly and peaceful personal lives, are nonetheless militarists if they explicitly or implicitly support a military system that, according to Holmes, guarantees war and risks eventual human extinction. By focusing on the two alternatives of pacifism and militarism, Holmes can help the Christian pacifist to think clearly about the greatest conceivable being: Would such a being *permit* the mass destruction of contemporary war if it could be prevented? Would such a being *approve* of war even if it were not within divine control to omnipotently manipulate the clash of creaturely freedoms? To both questions the pacifist should give a negative response. A straightforward simplification of our moral alternatives tends to simplify the ways in which we can view divine excellence. This is simplification in the good sense of the term whereby we can see more simply, and hence more clearly, what omnibenevolence means, and whereby our imitation of divinity entails an opposition to all violence, even if such violence is for the cause of liberating oppressed peoples.[17] The trick is for the Christian pacifist to avoid a retreat into quietism or quaint sectarianism and to promote a Gandhian–Martin Luther King-like refusal to kill as part of a method for making real social change and for making real progress in the contemplative life.

THE

COUNTERATTACK

BY JUST WAR

THEORISTS

As CAN BE expected, Christian opponents to pacifism will not stand idly by while the pacifist delivers a funeral oration for the just war theory. In fact, in the recent past there have been two significant efforts to have the bones of this theory resurrected and then trained for a counterattack on pacifism. The first of these is George Weigel's *Tranquillitas Ordinis*.[1] Weigel's overall thesis is that since 1965 there has been an abandonment on the part of Christian thinkers, in general, and Catholic thinkers, in particular (especially the American Catholic bishops), of the tradition of *tranquillitas ordinis*, the Augustinian tradition of peace through rationally ordered (tranquil) political community, a tradition that is integrally tied to the just war theory.

This abandonment, he thinks, is due to the desire to avoid at all costs the fire of contemporary war, but at the price of ignoring the pit of totalitarianism. By "totalitarianism" Weigel means communism only, in that the second world war, he thinks, signaled the defeat of right-wing totalitarianism. In fact, he sees quite a moral gap between current right-wing dictatorships and the far worse communist states. He concludes that we must be prepared to either engage in war or end up in a gulag.

As should now be obvious, it is not my intent to defend the Soviet Union against Weigel's criticisms. One only wishes that Weigel were more even-handed in his approach. If it is correct, as he alleges, that "socialist" states tend toward tyranny and are anti-democratic, it should nonetheless be noted that the Scandanavian countries are notable exceptions and that there are at least a few examples of left-wing governments that have been elected to office in democratic elections, but American forces, presumably with Weigel's approval, have helped to overthrow them (for example, Allende's Chile and Arbenz's Guatemala). Weigel is also correct that there is little point to paralleling America's history of civil liberties with the traditional denial of civil liberties in the Soviet Union (although blacks and Native Americans could, quite understandably, disagree with me here).[2] But might it be the case that in foreign policy there is significant room for drawing such a parallel? Soviet behavior in Afghanistan was atrocious; was America's behavior in Vietnam less so? The Soviet Union for several decades had a stranglehold on Eastern Europe; but is it sheer anti-American prejudice on the part of virtually every European intellectual to think that American hegemony in Central America has been every bit as severe?

Weigel is also on solid ground in criticizing the deterministic view of history that Marxism has traditionally fostered;[3] but quite ironically, despite the fact that capitalism is supposed to foster an open-ended future, it is common to have key decisions made in capitalist countries on the grounds of financial exigency and attended by the language of duress (which is also the language of the just war theory and of realism). And Weigel correctly points out Soviet brutality in shooting down the Korean Airlines civilians.[4] One wonders, however, whether Weigel would be willing to criticize American brutality in shooting down an Iranian civilian flight in 1988. In short, I think we should take with several grains of salt those attempts to resurrect just war theory because of "the pit of totalitarianism" in that these attempts are more likely due to a biased nationalism.

In fairness to Weigel it should be noted that he does not claim moral certitude in his defense of just war theory, but offers a defense laced with irony, an irony that he thinks is necessary if we (along with Albert Camus) want to avoid being either executioners or victims. Can we avoid the former, however, in contemporary war? I concur with Weigel's rejection of emotivism regarding issues in war and peace,[5] but his rational defense of irony has some untoward consequences, not the least of which, from the perspective of Christian pacifism, is his denigration of New Testament morality. In effect, Weigel grants the case I made in Chapter One and then indicates its irrelevance. Another consequence is his willingness to ally himself with (right-wing) tyrants who fall just short of the totalitarian pit.

Despite Weigel's intent to defend Christian tradition, his position is actually evidence of its abandonment. He is an obvious defender of *jus ad bellum*, but he conveniently gives little attention to *jus in bello*. He is quick to point out that Augustine was reluctant to elaborate on *jus in bello*,[6] but he fails to mention Aquinas's lack of such reluctance.[7] Weigel holds that the move from early Christian pacifism to just war theory was a theological Rubicon (contra Ramsey's claim that this move was a change of tactics only) and that we cannot return to primitive Christianity's eschatological hopes. Weigel may be right about such hopes, but unfortunately his criticisms of those who want to repristinize the Church are used to criticize as well defenders of *jus in bello*.

Weigel's own version of *jus in bello* is incredibly short and crudely utilitarian and is an attenuated and inaccurate rendering of the principle of double effect: the good obtained by war must outweigh the evils of the war.[8] And such a weighing is the job of legitimate authorities and not individual soldiers,[9] thereby relieving soldiers of the burdens of conscience and, I might add, thereby practically delivering an imprimatur to *jus in bello* violations. Along with almost all contemporary just war theorists, including John Courtney Murray, Weigel is comfortable with the soldier's reluctance to use too little force, but is annoyed instead with the "moralist's" tendency to prohibit too much force.[10] Although Weigel does not slide all the way toward General Sherman's end of the spectrum, he comes rather close: the primary issue in just war theory is not the problem of which weapons are used (or how they are used), but rather the issue of just cause.[11] Hence he is a just war theorist who at least leans toward realism (as did Murray) if he does not actually tumble into it headlong.

No doubt Weigel is correct in pointing out that guerrilla fighters, by using the civilian population as cover, themselves threaten innocent people.[12] But then Weigel goes on to plead for a "more sophisticated" connection between *jus ad bellum* and *jus in bello* so as to allow anti-guerrilla fighters to do their job.[13] One suspects that this "more sophisticated" position is one whereby *jus in bello* practically drops out of sight altogether. Weigel even seems to be in favor of defending, in certain circumstances, the use of precisely targeted nuclear weapons.

It is easy to understand why Weigel is upset by the recent statements on war and peace made by the American Catholic bishops. Weigel insists that they should have engaged in the sort of activities that preoccupied them before the Vietnam war, activities that, on Weigel's own admission, prevented them from questioning even the *jus in bello* practices of the Allies at the end of World War II, including the demand for unconditional surrender and the bombing of Dresden and Hiroshima. Weigel shows his ignorance of the stringency of traditional *jus in bello* restrictions when he assumes that the recent activities of the bishops are largely due to extra-theological factors, even the activities of conservative figures like John Cardinal Krol or Father Hesburgh.[14] Although Weigel is correct that there is a need for Christians to agree on at least some basic principles regarding war and peace,[15] he underestimates how important it is (on the most traditional grounds of just war theory itself, not to mention pacifism) that we agree that it is wrong to knowingly kill innocent people.

Weigel is quite explicit in his support for Ramsey's Protestant views (see Chapter One), views that are in the Augustinian tradition. This tradition acts as a counterweight, he thinks, to the contemporary tendency toward Pelagianism. This tendency, exhibited, for example, by Pope John XXIII, empties *tranquillitas ordinis* of "realism." It is too optimistic regarding what (sinful) human beings can accomplish, he thinks.[16] Along with a rejection of Pelagianism Weigel rejects those varieties of pacifism that psychologize peace by claiming that there cannot be peace among nations until our own hearts are pure and we have no animosity in us.[17] Weigel may (unwittingly) be correct here. There is a great deal of room for human beings to disagree with, even hate, each other without killing each other as well as killing innocent bystanders.

Weigel, like Anscombe (treated in Chapter One), does not view pacifism as a legitimate alternative to just war theory in Christianity[18] (an incredible view when the New Testament is considered) because pacifism is largely a non-intellectual position, he thinks, with no developed theory to support it.[19] Perhaps he should read the works in the modest bibliography at the end of this book. A problem appears, however, when Weigel claims that pacifist *theory* conflicts with just war theory such that no synthesis between the two can be forged. Such a conflict presupposes that there is a developed theory to support pacifism. His overall view is that *the* heritage of Christianity is embodied in just war theory and that this heritage should not be abandoned. Nor should Christians run to the contemporary political scene as breathless latecomers in that there is the Thomistic past to rely on,[20] Weigel thinks, even if he himself is not much aware of exactly what that tradition includes.

Pacifists are correctly warned by Weigel that if they are to be consistent they cannot support third world revolutions, that their acts of civil disobedience must show some sense of civic responsibility (that is, they must indeed be civil), and that they must be concerned not only with peace (or justice) but also with freedom. It is doubtful, however, if they could learn much from him regarding the evils of unilateral disarmament,[21] especially regarding his refusal to distinguish between unilateral disarmament and a unilateral initiative to reduce armaments by a certain percentage.

As before, Weigel makes it difficult for us to tell if his defense of the just war theory is a ruse for his patriotism. Pacifists are understandably a bit skittish of scholars like Weigel who are fond of the American Enterprise Institute (which only hires scholars who are frankly willing to deliver an apologia for right-wing political economy) or who see the automobile as an expression of spiritual creativity.[22] Weigel quite explicitly calls for a new defense of national patriotism[23] (like George Bush's fetish for the Pledge of Allegiance?) and seems overly worried that pacifists would put American violence on a par with that of the Nazis (he seems to think that most pacifists spell the word "Amerika"). To counteract pacifist extremism Weigel even doubts that there is such a thing as a military-industrial(-academic) complex,[24] a phrase that he always puts in quotation marks. These doubts can easily be allayed by looking at the percentage of the American gross national product taken up by defense expenditures and by civilian companies that rely for their health on defense expenditures. Similar connections can be found in almost all of the industrialized (or post-industrialized) nations of the world. Weigel should reread what Eisenhower said about this complex.

Weigel indirectly helps to make the case for the pragmatic death of the just war theory when he opens the floodgates of support for *his* country's violence: It would have been a good idea, Weigel thinks, to initiate bombing of China's nuclear plants because "intervention is in the nature of things" (what things?).[25] Israel was correct in bombing such plants in Iraq.[26] Intervention is legitimate to protect our (note the possessive) oil in the Mideast.[27] There was no ambiguity in the Granada invasion (and no mention of the bombed mental hospital).[28] We should support "democratization" in Chile under Augusto Pinochet because Salvador Allende, whom we helped to overthrow, was not a democrat (even though he came to power in a fair election).[29] There is no parallel between what was Soviet domination of Eastern Europe and American domination of Central America; in fact, we should have given more support to Napoleon Duarte's "Christian Democracy" in El Salvador (despite the fact that under his rule 40,000 people, mostly civilians, were killed with American weapons).[30] Ronald Reagan's

Central America policies in the 1980s differed in kind from more brutal American policies in the 1920s; the contras constituted a democratic opposition in Nicaragua (forget the fact that they had a tendency to kill villagers), and *La Prensa* should have been kept alive, even by force, as the free press of Nicaragua (although Weigel makes no notice that there is no free press whatsoever in El Salvador or Guatemala).

And so on. It is not just Weigel's American patriotism in particular that is bothersome. In general he has a bias in favor of Western European civilization, as is evidenced in his refusal to admit that imperial rivalry had anything to do with the origin of World War I.[31] He seems to think that Christians have turned against the West because of the legacy of those like Daniel Berrigan. But one wonders if Berrigan has the influence Weigel alleges in that he has been "disinvited" from speaking even at the campuses of his own Jesuit order.[32]

Not surprisingly Weigel is an apologist for America's involvement in Vietnam. He thinks the solution to the problem in Vietnam would have been free elections,[33] but he does not mention the fact that the United States prevented United Nations-sponsored elections in 1956 for fear that Ho Chi Minh would have won. Hence Weigel reifies North and South Vietnam as two separate realities. He makes no mention of the daily killing of non-combatants by the United States in the Vietnam war. In fact, he even tries to diminish the importance of the notorious bombings of North Vietnamese cities. His claim is that there were *some* violations of *jus in bello*, but these are not terribly bothersome because the American bombers were under stricter standards than ever before.[34] I hope I have shown that the relevant standards of *jus in bello* were neither invented nor applied in 1968, but have been around at least since Saint Thomas Aquinas. For Weigel, 1968 was a chaotic, dreadful year not because the United States was bombing villages, but because those protesting the war were not civil.[35]

Weigel should be commended for requesting civil debate, but his criticisms of the protesters can carry weight only if they are concomitant with criticisms of the lies of Lyndon Johnson and Richard Nixon.

In short, if progress is to be made in debates between Christian pacifists and just war theorists it is imperative that just war theorists make it clearer than Weigel has that they are, in fact, defending just war theory and not their own nationalistic prejudices. James Schall[36] is one just war theorist who is like Weigel in defending just war theory, including nuclear deterrence, without even mentioning that such a defense entails the intention to kill innocents. But these positions provide the absolute nadir. Somewhat more tolerable are the views of William O'Brien, George Mavrodes, and Joseph Nye,[37] who reject discrimination (between combatants and non-combatants) as an absolute principle, but leave indeterminate the issue as to *how* one can ever claim that knowingly killing innocent people can be morally permissible. O'Brien, however, unintentionally aids the pacifist's case by admitting that contemporary war requires the violation of an absolute principle of discrimination.

It is important for pacifists to be able to make judgments among the different expressions of just war theory so as to indicate which among them most closely approximates the goal of real peace. For example, a statement made by the Catholic bishops of France in 1983[38] is unacceptable to pacifists. The bishops claim that nuclear deterrence is an evil, but because it is the lesser of two evils it can be tolerated. G. R. Dunstan and Michael Novak hold a similar view.[39] Not only does this position conflict with the Council of Trent, where it was claimed that one is never forced to knowingly do evil (note again the Socratic belief that one can be forced to receive evil but not to do it);[40] it also strips Christian morality of its distinctiveness and its intellectual force. Less bothersome is the view of W. D.

Ross, who holds that not killing the innocent is a prima facie duty, but it is a duty that can be overridden by other considerations.[41] It should be noted, however, that Ross is here, like Walzer, open to the charge of being a utilitarian of extremity in the guise of Kantian clothing. Ross, and especially Walzer, should be more forthright about the utilitarian grounding of their theories.

Some earlier just war theorists, as we have seen, contain implicitly the pacifist position. For example, Fathers Roh and John Ford, in their forceful defenses of the ideas that a good end does not justify an evil means and that there has been unanimity of opinion (until recently) in Christianity regarding discrimination as an absolute principle, reinforce my thesis in this book.[42] Reinforcement is also offered by John Finnis, Joseph Boyle, and Germain Grisez in a book that I would like to examine in detail in this Epilogue.[43] That is, I wish to show that not all just war theorists are, like Weigel, anathema to pacifists, thus leaving open some room for continued dialogue between pacifists and just war theorists.

Unlike Weigel's book, the book by Finnis, Boyle, and Grisez is to be commended for having just war theory confront head-on the issue of the killing of innocents. The "common morality" of Christianity, and of the Western tradition in general, they think, excludes killing the innocent, and excludes threatening to kill the innocent in deterrence theory, where "city swapping" and "final retaliation" are the lingua franca.[44] The authors clearly locate "intention" as part of the plan on which one freely acts,[45] thereby prohibiting any slippery use of the term that would permit the killing of innocents in war, with "innocents" referring to those who could not be used to verify the proposition "that society is at war with us."[46] It must be granted that this definition, as with any other, leaves certain borderline cases, but it is sufficient to protect the majority of citizens in modern nation states.

The authors prohibit nuclear deterrence largely because of their (correct) claim that targeting does not define intent. That is, one cannot aim a nuclear weapon at a military installation ten miles outside a city and still maintain that one killed the civilians inside the city unintentionally. What we threaten to do is what we want the other side to fear because of our threats, and in this case the other side obviously fears city swapping or final retaliation.[47] One must regard the statement of deterrence theory by French political and military leaders as perversely admirable in that they openly admit that their policy is anti-city. The British articulation of their threat is a bit more coy, and the United States policy, at least since the 1970s, has included a disavowal of targeting cities as such.[48] The authors ably dismantle the sophistry of British and American justifications of deterrence theory. That is, their threats are the same as those of the French, only more powerful.

The pacifist can also receive solace from the authors' criticisms of other devices that some just war theorists use: that "mere possession" of nuclear weapons does not constitute a threat to an opponent; that it is possible to keep deterrence theory as an option if we do not intend to use nuclear weapons on the day of reckoning; that deterrence theory can be moral as long as the threat to use nuclear weapons is a bluff; that targeting determines intention;[49] and that a Strategic Defense Initiative that claims to develop a purely defensive weapon can hardly be seen as having developed a counterforce weapon only, because it would give its sole possessor a war-winning capability.[50] The aggressive nature of the Star Wars plan is amplified by the fact that almost everyone outside the United States sees it as a violation of the 1972 Anti-Ballistic Missile Treaty.

Non-combatant immunity has been taken for granted in Christianity because it is so central to the tradition.[51] Data that are only sometimes present (for example, bright red) are easier to perceive than data that are ubiquitous (for example, spatial extension). Hence a lackadaisical attitude has arisen in recent decades, a situation exploited by utilitarians like Gregory Kavka.[52] But the authors demonstrate the futility of accurate utilitarian calculations regarding the probability of nuclear war. C. P. Snow was incorrect in his 1960 claim that nuclear weapons would certainly be used within ten years.[53] Is there really much stronger evidence to support Herman Kahn's claim that the probability of nuclear war is "very, very low"?[54] And what is the foundation against which we can judge the legitimacy of the thesis that the probability of nuclear war under the present system of deterrence is less than the assurance of Soviet domination if we did not have a system of deterrence?[55] What is surprising is that some develop this thesis while admitting that the client states of the United States are in no better shape than those of the Soviet Union.[56]

In short, consequentialist arguments regarding the legitimacy or illegitimacy of nuclear deterrence must fail because the future is the region of the indeterminate.[57] Because it is not here yet we cannot know it in detail, but can only develop the sort of educated guesses I offered in Chapter Seven. An intelligent moral agent can know past actualities as actual—they indeed have happened—and can know future contingencies as contingent. To indicate knowledge of a future contingency as an actuality, as all consequentialist arguments regarding nuclear weapons must do, including utilitarian arguments, is, quite simply, to feign knowledge one does not have.

Finnis, Boyle, and Grisez are also very instructive regarding the facile claim that one need not disarm immediately once one realizes that nuclear deterrence is immoral. In that there is no moral justification for an interim deterrence that is more convincing than the moral justification of deterrence itself, the moral thing to do, as the pacifist has always urged, is to unilaterally disarm.[58] It must be admitted that if immorality is done it is better that it be mild rather than severe; hence it makes sense for a woman to encourage her enraged husband to only spank a child rather than to beat him with a club. But this encouragement is not to be construed as a defense of the morality of spanking.[59] So also, if pacifists tolerate deterrence while the process of disarmament is occurring (a process that is not to be confused with dismantling a few weapons here while building several more over there), this tolerance should not be confused with a *moral* defense of deterrence.[60] As our authors correctly point out, morality's demands do not wait.[61]

Although Finnis, Boyle, and Grisez develop a just war theory that is far more palatable to a pacifist than Weigel's, there are nonetheless serious problems with their views. They explicitly ally themselves with Anscombe's views on just war theory,[62] views that I have criticized in Chapter One. No doubt they are correct that many who advocate unilateral disarmament are, as they put it, naive, gullible, and duplicitous regarding the Soviet Union,[63] but to admit this is not to refute George F. Kennan's thesis (mentioned earlier in this book), which they think they have done.[64] This thesis suggests that even if the Soviet Union is brutal within its borders there is no necessary connection between such brutality and the claim that their foreign policy is largely motivated by (a quite understandable, if not justifiable) fear of the West.

"Common morality" (that is, the traditional morality of Christianity) does not, as they seem to think,[65] require us to oppose the Soviets militarily if only we could do so without killing innocents. Nor does it require us to say that unilateral disarmament will "probably" mean Soviet domination of us,[66] especially because of the authors' own criticisms of consequentialism.

At times the authors come dangerously close to backing off from their defense of discrimination as an absolute principle. For example, when they claim that "one need not intend what one's behavior causes others to fear,"[67] as in buying a nasty dog whose behavior scares off burglers, they run the risk of encouraging a misuse of the principle of double effect, a misuse quite popular among just war theorists and war is hell theorists. But even their own carefully reasoned use of Aquinas's principle of double effect assumes without argument that there are, in fact, contemporary wars where innocents are not killed. Just one or two examples from them of such wars from twentieth-century history would have been helpful. Further, pacifists would have continued doubts regarding the claim that the killing of combatants in war is only a foreseen side effect, as opposed to a direct choice to kill human beings, a choice that the authors admit is immoral.[68]

It should now be obvious, however, that even more bothersome to the pacifist than the killing of combatants (although even this is morally bothersome) is the killing of innocents (or, again, if the reader prefers, non-combatants or civilians). Almost always the authors condemn the killing of innocents, but what are we to make of the thesis that the foreseen killing of the innocent "may be accepted only if it will be a side-effect of acts whose precise object not only does not include their death but excludes every purpose to harm them. It may be accepted, in short, only as incidental to the force used against combatants to thwart their unjust challenge."[69] As far as I can tell, this thesis flatly contradicts the major aim of *Nuclear Deterrence, Morality and Realism*. The authors stretch their criticisms of nuclear weapons to the breaking point when they say that it is legitimate to retain very small nuclear weapons for (supposedly) purely defensive purposes—for example, to use against submarines or to defend a mountain pass.[70] It strikes me that allowing such weapons requires as a necessary condition the claim that targeting defines intention, a claim that, as we have seen, the authors would otherwise want to reject.

Finnis, Boyle, and Grisez, however, unlike Weigel, offer some grounds for hope that just war theorists will eventually be seduced by the allure of pacifist *reasoning*, a seduction intimated when the authors admit that past arms races always reached the finish line at the next war.[71] But the present arms race, if something like Armageddon is avoided, can only be an endless (and hence immoral, in that the *goal* of just war theory is supposed to be peace) Marathon.

NOTES

Preface

1. Peter Brock, *Pacifism in Europe to 1914* (Princeton, N.J.: Princeton University Press, 1972). Brock's work forms the backbone of Jenny Teichman's chapter titled "The Origins of Pacifism" in *Pacifism and the Just War* (New York: Blackwell, 1986); see Chapter Six.

2. See the famous passages in Kant's *Groundwork for the Metaphysics of Morals* and Mill's *Utilitarianism*. Both works can can be found in Steven Cahn, ed., *Classics of Western Philosophy* (Indianapolis: Hackett, 1977).

3. On the differences between Greek-Roman and Judeo-Christian (particularly Christian) ethics see Paul Carrick, *Medical Ethics in Antiquity* (Boston: Reidel, 1985).

4. Richard Wasserstrom, in his essay "On the Morality of War: A Preliminary Inquiry," in Wasserstrom, ed., *War and Morality* (Los Angeles: Wadsworth, 1970), notes that Catholic moralists had, until the 1960s, dominated thought about war and peace issues, but not because there was a paucity of wars to think about.

Chapter One

1. A. J. P. Taylor, *The Origins of the Second World War* (New York: Atheneum, 1962). I will return to Taylor's book later to show that the popular reading of his thesis that follows is in one important respect inadequate. Also see the essays on Taylor in Esmonde Robertson, ed., *The Origins of the Second World War* (London: Macmillan, 1971).

2. Characteristically, Nietzsche offers other passages that make his extreme stance seem extreme in the other direction.

3. Saint Thomas Aquinas, *Summa Theologiae* (Blackfriars ed.; New York: McGraw-Hill, 1972), 2a2ae, 40, 1. Parenthetical citations in the text are to this work.

4. It should be noted that most Christians today reject this double standard by accepting modern theories of the right of self-defense in criminal law.

5. Also see Aquinas, *Summa Theologiae* 2a2ae, 29, 2, and Saint Thomas Aquinas, *Summa Contra Gentiles* (Blackfriars ed.; New York: McGraw-Hill, 1972), III, 34.

6. G. E. M. Anscombe, "War and Murder," in James Rachels, ed., *Moral Problems*, 3rd ed. (New York: Harper and Row, 1979); also found in Anscombe's *Collected Philosophical Papers* (Minneapolis: University of Minnesota Press, 1981).

7. The principle of double effect is the idea that an action may have two effects: one desired and the other foreseen but in no way desired. In the case of war, one could desire to defend the innocent, while foreseeing that one would kill in the process without desiring to kill. It will become obvious in this book that I am very much opposed to using the principle of double effect to justify the killing of innocent people in war. It will also become obvious that I am opposed (on Kantian grounds, among others) to the use of this principle to justify the killing of an enemy soldier, even in a war with *jus ad bellum*. But in the latter case it is more understandable (if not justifiable) to try to use this principle to legitimate the deliberate killing of a human being. It might be legitimately asked, however, whether pacifists must use the principle of double effect in spite of themselves in order to justify inflicting any pain

in any context, for example in the dentist's chair or in the effort to incarcerate criminals. It is correct to say that in order to justify the dentist's activity we need to say that the dentist intends to benefit the patient, but that in this effort she foresees but does not intend that she will cause pain. The crucial factors to notice, however, are that the dentist has the consent of the patient and can, in principle, be reconciled to the patient as an autonomous human subject after the dental treatment. As we will see, the same can also be true (but often is not) with respect to the criminal. To the objection that the pain caused to the relatives of the criminal by his incarceration needs justification, I would respond that it is not we who need to apologize to these relatives but the criminal. That is, by humane incarceration *we* are not harming innocent relatives. Humane incarceration, although it may not have the consent of the criminal, does require the possibility that we will receive such consent eventually because of our conciliatory efforts. These conditions cannot be met if we maim or kill our opponent.

8. Unlike Anscombe, most modern Christian defenders of the just war limit their theories to *defensive* warfare, although some (for example, Michael Walzer) find preemptive strikes acceptable.

9. Anscombe also says, "How false is the conception of Christ's teaching as *correcting* the religion of the ancient Israelites, and substituting a higher and more 'spiritual' religion for theirs." Clearly she cannot have her cake and eat it too.

10. On Jesus's remark about the fall of a sparrow see my *Hartshorne and the Metaphysics of Animal Rights* (Albany: State University of New York Press, 1988).

11. Paul Ramsey, *War and the Christian Conscience* (Durham, N.C.: Duke University Press, 1961), pp. xv–xvii.

12. Paul Ramsey, *The Just War* (New York: Scribner's, 1968), pp. 500–501, 523.

13. Thomas Kuhn, *The Structure of Scientific Revolutions* (2nd ed.; Chicago: University of Chicago Press, 1970), chaps. 2–3. Some may want to maintain the just war paradigm by appealing to Aquinas at question 64, article 8, where it is claimed that there is nothing immoral when someone (even an innocent person) is killed *accidentally*; but, as we will see later in this book, to kill

accidentally after we have taken due care not to harm innocents is quite different from killing innocents unintentionally (albeit knowingly) under the rubric of double effect. My claim is that this latter sort of killing is neither morally commendable nor morally permissible. If due care is taken to protect innocents, it may well be that killing them in a true accident is amoral.

Chapter Two

1. See a wonderful literary portrayal of Jesus as a pacifist in Nikos Kazantzakis, *The Odyssey: A Modern Sequel*, trans. Kimon Friar (New York: Simon and Schuster, 1958), bk. 21.

2. Warren Steinkraus, "Does It Make Any Sense to Talk About a 'Just War'?" *Journal of Social Philosophy* 5 (Jan. 1974): 8–11.

3. Saint Thomas Aquinas, *Summa Theologiae* (Blackfriars ed.; New York: McGraw-Hill, 1972), 2a2ae, 40, 1. Parenthetical citations are to this work.

4. More work needs to be done on Aquinas's erotetic logic— that is, the logic of question and answer—where certain questions dictate which answers are logically possible. Just war theorists in particular should pay more attention to Aquinas's erotetic logic. Some questions already presuppose answers: Have you stopped beating your wife yet? Is it always a sin to wage war?

5. See John Ford's classic study, "The Morality of Oblitera-tion Bombing," *Theological Studies* 5 (1944): 261–309; also in Richard Wasserstrom, ed., *War and Morality* (Los Angeles: Wads-worth, 1970). I admit that, strictly speaking, the combatant–non-combatant distinction is not exactly the same as the guilty–innocent distinction. First, not all combatants are guilty—say, if they have been lied to by their political leaders regarding the conditions of *jus ad bellum* or *jus in bello* or if they have been conscripted under duress. And, second, many non-combatants are not innocent—say, if they earnestly wish victory for their side against the "enemy." Nonetheless I do not think much harm is done by conflating these distinctions because, on the criteria of

the just war theory itself, combatants are "guilty" in the sense that they can legitimately be killed in a war with a just cause, and because, even if there are fewer innocent people than non-combatants in modern war, there are still an enormous number of innocent people in any nation who ought not to be killed. Even non-combatants who are hardly innocent ought not to be killed and hence are, in a minimal sense, "innocent."

6. This example is loosely based on a passage from Paul Ramsey, *War and the Christian Conscience* (Durham, N.C.: Duke University Press, 1961), although Ramsey would not agree with the conclusion I draw.

7. See George F. Kennan, *The Nuclear Delusion* (New York: Pantheon, 1983).

8. George Weigel, "The Catholics and the Arms Race: A Primer for the Perplexed," *Chicago Studies* 18 (1979): 169–195.

9. National Conference of Catholic Bishops, *The Challenge of Peace: God's Promise and Our Response* (Washington, D.C., May 3, 1983).

10. See James Childress, "Just-War Criteria," in Thomas Shannon, ed., *War or Peace? The Search for New Answers* (Maryknoll, N.Y.: Orbis, 1980). Childress is a just war theorist who agrees that the prima facie duty not to kill puts the burden of proof not on the pacifist but on the just war theorist, who would like to override this duty. In order to do so, however, just war theorists must weigh the criteria of their theory, which they can do in one of five ways. (1) They can say that the inability to meet any of the criteria renders a war unjust. (2) They can say that the criteria themselves establish prima facie duties that can be overridden by more stringent duties. (3) They can say that several criteria of the theory must be met, but no single criterion is required for a war to be just. (4) They can say that the criteria are merely "rules of thumb" and do not prescribe what we ought to do. Or (5) They can say that the criteria must be arranged in order of importance so that the most important must be met before the second can be considered and so on.

Childress is correct that the burden of proof is on the just war theorists, but options 3 and 4 are so vague as to be practically useless. Option 5 really is a version of option 2 because the criteria at the bottom of Childress's lexical ordering in option 5 are in effect prima facie duties that can be overridden. Hence, our choice, as I have indicated in different language, is between options 1 and 2. The present book is an attempt to defend option 1 as constituting what a just war would be like if there were one. A problem with Childress's option 2 is that it establishes a cumbersome layering of prima facie duties: first a prima facie duty not to kill, which is overridden by a prima facie duty not to kill innocent people, which in turn can be overridden, and so on. Eventually one must wonder whether the concept of duty really means anything at all to just war theorists.

11. See James Turner Johnson, *Ideology, Reason, and the Limitations of War: Religious and Secular Concepts, 1200–1740* (Princeton, N.J.: Princeton University Press, 1975); *Just War Tradition and the Restraint of War: A Moral and Historical Inquiry* (Princeton, N.J.: Princeton University Press, 1981); "Historical Tradition and Moral Judgment: The Case of Just War Tradition," *Journal of Religion* 64 (1984): 299–317; and *Can Modern War Be Just?* (New Haven, Conn.: Yale University Press, 1984).

12. Johnson, "Historical Tradition," p. 300.

13. Alfred Vanderpol, *La doctrine scholastique du droit de guerre* (Paris: Pedone, 1919).

14. Johnson, *Ideology, Reason, and Limitations*, pp. 25, 39, 40, 171.

15. Ibid., pp. 42, 44.

16. Ibid., p. 43.

17. Ibid., p. 44.

18. Ibid., pp. 34, 75, 150. Also see Johnson, "Historical Tradition," pp. 305–306.

19. Johnson, "Historical Tradition," p. 301.

20. Ibid., p. 311.

21. Ibid., p. 314.

22. Ibid., pp. 311, 315.

23. Johnson, *Just War Tradition*, pp. 9–10.

24. Ibid., pp. 105, 175.

25. Johnson, "Historical Tradition," pp. 312–313. Also see Johnson, *Can Modern War Be Just?* p. 12.

26. Frederick Russell, *The Just War in the Middle Ages* (Cambridge, Eng.: Cambridge University Press, 1975), pp. 264, 273–274.

27. Likewise, if a judge knows that an innocent person is being convicted, she should question the witnesses all the more searchingly. But if she cannot free the person, the judge is not guilty; rather, the guilt lies with those who allege the innocent person's guilt. See Aquinas, *Summa Theologiae*, 2a2ae, 64, 6. Again, Aquinas is clearer here than Johnson and Russell indicate, and more consistent.

28. See Russell, *Just War*, pp. 274–275.

29. National Conference of Catholic Bishops, *Challenge of Peace*, pp. vii, 101, n. 8.

30. Ibid., p. 25.

31. Ibid., p. 33.

32. Ibid., p. 47.

33. Ibid., pp. iii, 34.

34. Ibid., p. 61.

35. Ibid., p. 57.

36. Donald Wells, *War Crimes and Laws of War* (Lanham, Md.: University Press of America, 1984). Although I have often used the innocent-guilty distinction interchangeably with the non-combatant–combatant distinction, Wells more often uses the latter, and with some good reason, as we have seen above. Many non-combatants may not be totally "innocent" if they voted, say, for a war party; and one can legitimately doubt if conscripted soldiers are really "guilty." But, as before, generally speaking I do not think that any harm is done by using these distinctions interchangeably.

Chapter Three

1. See Michael Walzer, *Just and Unjust Wars* (New York: Basic Books, 1977), esp. pp. 3–5, 10–11, 13, 25, 28–32, 136, 229–231, 325, and Richard Wasserstrom, "On the Morality of War: A Pre-

liminary Inquiry," in Wasserstrom, ed., *War and Morality* (Los Angeles: Wadsworth, 1970), pp. 78–82. I have freely borrowed from these two authors throughout this chapter.

2. Walzer, *Just and Unjust Wars*, pp. 10–11.

3. Ibid., p. 28.

4. Ibid., p. 30.

5. Ibid., p. 32.

6. Wasserstrom, "On the Morality of War," pp. 78–82.

7. Ibid., pp. 86, 94–101. I should note once again that of the three general positions regarding the morality of war (war is hell, just war, and pacifism) only two have been acceptable in Christianity (just war and pacifism); yet this is purposely to ignore the notion of a divinely sanctioned crusade, popular in the Middle Ages but (thankfully) not so today (cf. the jihad in contemporary Islam). Because of the supposed divine sanction for a crusade such a fight is quite different from human efforts to justify war.

8. Walzer, *Just and Unjust Wars*, p. 329.

9. See, for example, Gene Sharp, *Exploring Nonviolent Alternatives* (Boston: Porter Sargent, 1971).

10. Walzer, *Just and Unjust Wars*, p. 330.

11. Ibid., p. 331.

12. Ibid., p. 334.

13. Ibid., p. xi.

14. Ibid., p. 325.

15. Ibid., p. 326.

Chapter Four

1. Iris Murdoch, *The Fire and the Sun* (Oxford: Clarendon, 1977).

2. An illustration of this mosaic can be found in Pal Kelemen, *El Greco Revisited* (New York: Macmillan, 1961).

3. See Millard Meiss, *The Great Age of Fresco* (New York: Braziller, 1970).

4. See R. H. Wilenski, *Flemish Painters, 1430–1830* (New York: Viking, 1960), vol. 2.

5. See Kelemen, *El Greco Revisited*. In addition to the El Grecos listed below, sixteenth-century versions include two in the Wallace Collection in London: an Italian bowl and a French enamel.

6. For example, in the Frick Collection in New York, the National Gallery in London, the Cook Collection in Richmond, and the Minneapolis Institute of Arts. See Kelemen, *El Greco Revisited*, and Antonia Valentin, *El Greco* (Garden City, N.Y.: Doubleday, 1955).

7. Valentin, *El Greco*, p. 45.

8. See Wilenski, *Flemish Painters*. This painting is now in Antwerp.

9. See Richard Spear, *Caravaggio and His Followers* (New York: Harper and Row, 1975). The Cavallino is in the National Gallery in London.

10. This painting is found in the Pushkin Museum in Moscow. See A. Bredius, *Rembrandt: The Complete Edition of the Paintings* (London: Phaidon, 1969).

11. Giordano's work, now in Naples, can be seen in Ellis Waterhouse, *Italian Baroque Painting* (Greenwich, Conn.: Phaidon, 1962).

12. See Murdoch, *Fire and Sun*, pp. 70–71. The following phrases in quotation marks come from Murdoch.

13. The name of the pyrrhic dance alludes to its inventor, Pyrrichos, as well as to the fiery movements found in it. The dance of peace is also sometimes referred to as *eireniken*.

Chapter Five

1. J. O. Urmson, "Saints and Heroes," in A. I. Melden, ed., *Essays in Moral Philosophy* (Seattle: University of Washington Press, 1958), p. 198.

2. Ibid., pp. 200–201.

3. Not all supererogatory acts are heroic, however; for example, a person who voluntarily picks up the litter that other people have dropped is not a hero. Further, I realize that a full

treatment of heroic acts would have to include consideration of the motivation for those acts. The need for the category of supererogatory acts is seen when we try to place them elsewhere. They are certainly not prohibited, nor are they duties. To say that they are permissible leaves so much unexplained as to be misleading.

4. Urmson, "Saints and Heroes," p. 203.

5. Ibid., p. 209.

6. Ibid., p. 211.

7. Ibid., p. 212.

8. Ibid., p. 213.

9. Raghavan Iyer, *The Moral and Political Thought of Mahatma Gandhi* (Oxford: Oxford University Press, 1973), p. 4.

10. Ibid., p. 136 ff.

11. Ibid., p. 143.

12. Ibid., p. 165.

13. Ibid., p. 135.

14. Ibid., p. 210.

15. Ibid., pp. 5, 137.

16. Ibid., p. 48.

17. Ibid., p. 135.

18. Ibid., p. 143.

19. Ibid., p. 139.

20. Ibid., pp. 138, 144.

21. Ibid., p. 178.

22. Gandhi obviously did not intend these "concepts" to be rigorously defined or distinguished from each other; I am doing the best I can for my Western audience, which demands some sort of clarity.

23. Iyer, *Moral and Political Thought*, p. 184.

24. Saint Thomas Aquinas, *Summa Theologiae* (Blackfriar's ed.; New York: McGraw-Hill, 1972), 2a2ae, 64, 6.

25. Immanuel Kant, "Perpetual Peace," I, 6, in L. W. Beck, ed., *On History* (Indianapolis: Bobbs-Merrill, 1963).

26. M. K. Gandhi, *Non-Violence in Peace and War*, vol. 2 (Navajivan, 1949), p. 29.

27. Ibid., p. 94.

28. Ibid., p. 93.

29. Ibid., p. 90.

30. Ibid., p. 49.

31. Ibid., p. 93. In many ways the thesis I am developing in this chapter is a companion to the conception of tragedy developed by Arthur Miller in his *Death of a Salesman*. The egalitarian spirit of our age allows us to see common human beings as being as tragic as kings. So also with heroism or sainthood. Heroism in ancient Greece (for example, that of Odysseus) largely consisted in the military and sexual exploits of the aristocracy. In the Middle Ages sainthood was connected with divine grace and miracles. To equate heroism or sainthood with supererogation is, in a way, to continue this transcendent tradition, which should have been called into question when Beethoven took away his dedication to Napoleon from the Third Symphony, if not before, when Jesus was born among animals, lived with fishermen, and died on a cross. It should also be remembered that Socrates was a moral hero for Gandhi, perhaps a non-supererogatory one.

32. See John Ansbro, *Martin Luther King, Jr.: The Making of a Mind* (Maryknoll, N.Y.: Orbis, 1982).

33. Douglas Lackey, *The Ethics of War and Peace* (Englewood Cliffs, N.J.: Prentice-Hall, 1989), p. 2. The works that Lackey criticizes are Hans Morgenthau, *Politics Among Nations* (New York: Knopf, 1949); Henry Kissinger, "Force and Diplomacy in the Nuclear Age," *Foreign Affairs*, Apr. 1956; and Thomas Nagel, "Ruthlessness in Public Life," in Stuart Hampshire, ed., *Public and Private Morality* (Cambridge, Eng.: Cambridge University Press, 1978).

34. Ibid., p. 4.

35. Ibid., p. 9.

36. Ibid., p. 12.

37. Ibid., pp. 16–17.

38. On the varieties of pacifism Lackey relies on the work of Peter Brock—for example, *Twentieth Century Pacifism* (New York: Van Nostrand, 1976).

39. Lackey, *Ethics of War and Peace*, p. 24.

40. Ibid., p. 43.

41. Ibid., p. 52.

42. Ibid., p. 59.

43. Ibid., p. 60.

44. One defender of laws of war as conventional is George Mavrodes, in "Conventions and the Morality of War," *Philosophy and Public Affairs* 4 (1975): 117–131.

45. Lackey, *Ethics of War and Peace*, pp. 61–62.

46. Ibid., p. 65.

47. Ibid., p. 66.

48. Ibid., p. 67.

49. Lackey (incredibly) says that the distinction between direct and indirect killing was first developed by Bentham. See Chapter Two on Saint Thomas Aquinas.

50. Lackey, *Ethics of War and Peace*, p. 70.

51. Ibid., pp. 72–73.

52. Ibid., p. 80.

53. Ibid.

54. Ibid., p. 114.

55. Ibid., p. 120. As far as I can tell, Lackey's views are similar to those of James Sterba in "How to Achieve Nuclear Deterrence Without Threatening Nuclear Destruction," in Sterba, ed., *The Ethics of War and Nuclear Deterrence* (Los Angeles: Wadsworth, 1985), and of the United Methodist Council of Bishops in *In Defense of Creation* (Nashville: Graded Press, 1986).

56. Ibid., p. 123.

57. Ibid., pp. 129–130.

Chapter Six

1. See Michael Walzer, *Just and Unjust Wars* (New York: Basic Books, 1977), pp. 188–196. Also see Walzer's examples from the world wars, the Korean war, and so on.

2. *Time*, Nov. 14, 1983, pp. 23–24. With a nonchalance typical of our age, the *Time* writer calls the bombing of the mental hospital an "understandable error"—*a fortiori* the bombing of apartment buildings in Libya or Panama.

3. See George F. Kennan, *The Nuclear Delusion* (New York: Pantheon, 1983), pp. 3–4.

4. See the defense of Christian pacifism in Stanley Hauerwas, *Should War Be Eliminated?* (Milwaukee: Marquette University Press, 1984). Also see some historical notes on the nature of the medieval just war theory and its implications for contemporary warfare in the work of James Turner Johnson—for example, "Historical Tradition and Moral Judgment: The Case of Just War Tradition," *Journal of Religion* 64 (1984): 299–317.

5. See William James's famous essay "The Moral Equivalent of War," in Richard A. Wasserstrom, ed., *War and Morality* (Los Angeles: Wadsworth, 1970), for a justification of feisty resistance to evil as a legitimate form of pacifism. This feistiness might even be compatible with some uses of force, but not those reluctantly tolerated until "real" pacifism is practiced. These uses of force would have to be such that reconciliation was possible with the person coerced into not using violence on others—for example, through the use of sedative darts now used to capture wild animals. This use of force, perhaps compatible with pacifism, allows us to see why some pacifists defend position I instead of position H. That is, force may be used against evildoers, according to some pacifists, as long as it is meant to disarm and allows the possibility of reconciliation—in short, as long as the evildoer is not maimed or killed.

6. Jenny Teichman, *Pacifism and the Just War* (New York: Blackwell, 1986). See pp. 6–8 for Teichman's own classification of pacifisms.

7. Ibid., p. 2.

8. Ibid., p. 5.

9. Ibid., pp. 108–109.

10. Ibid., pp. 26–27.

11. Teichman also does a meticulous job of dismantling Jan Narveson's claim that the pacifist's response to violence is self-contradictory (ibid., pp. 29–37). See Jan Narveson, "Pacifism, a Philosophical Analysis," in Wasserstrom, ed., *War and Morality*, pp. 63–77. Another critic of Narveson is Michael Martin, "On an Argument Against Pacifism," *Philosophical Studies* 26 (Dec. 1974), pp. 437–442.

12. Teichman, *Pacifism and the Just War*, pp. 43–44.

13. Ibid., pp. 44, 63.

14. Ibid., p. 46.

15. For example, in the eight-year stretch when Frank Rizzo was mayor of Philadelphia, over sixty *unarmed* alleged criminals were killed by Philadelphia police.

16. Cf. Teichman, *Pacifism and the Just War*, p. 80.

17. Ibid., p. 43.

18. Ibid., pp. 53–54. See H. E. J. Cowdrey, "Bishop Ermenfried of Sion and the Penetential Ordinance Following the Battle of Hastings," *Journal of Ecclesiastical History* 20 (1969), pp. 225–242.

19. Teichman, *Pacifism and the Just War*, p. 58.

20. Ibid., p. 63.

21. Ibid., pp. 66–67.

22. Ibid., p. 75.

23. Ibid., p. 77.

24. Ibid., pp. 79–80.

25. Ibid., pp. 81–87.

26. Phillip Montague, in "Self-Defense and Choosing Between Lives," *Philosophical Studies* 40 (1981): 207–220, sees the right not to be killed and the obligation not to kill as being on a par, but he does not reach a pacifistic conclusion.

27. Teichman, *Pacifism and the Just War*, p. 101.

28. Ibid., p. 103.

29. Bernard Williams, *Moral Luck* (Cambridge, Eng.: Cambridge University Press, 1976).

30. Teichman, *Pacifism and the Just War*, pp. 104–105.

31. Ibid.

32. Ibid., p. 106.

33. Ibid., p. 107.

34. Teichman's book is full of interesting citations, however. For example, she alerts us (p. 116) to the crucial move made in just war theory in the Counter-Reformation by Francisco Suarez when he said that soldiers must go to war when ordered to do so even if it is possible that the war is unjust. And she also alerts us (p. 121) to one of the major defects in utilitarian calculations about war: by the time we learn if an action in war is right or wrong it will be

too late for our knowledge to affect conduct. As I have mentioned in this book, utilitarianism and just war theory are often more defective than pacifism on purely pragmatic grounds in that they cannot be used to guide conduct.

35. Teichman, *Pacifism and the Just War*, pp. 110–111.

36. Two other scholars who initially give support to pacifism, but then take it away, are Richard Norman, "The Case for Pacifism," *Journal of Applied Philosophy* 5 (1988): 197–210, and Tom Regan, "A Defense of Pacifism," *Canadian Journal of Philosophy* 2 (Sept. 1972): 73–86. The former defends pacifism on the grounds of (Kantian) respect for human life; these grounds provide not only plausible but very strong arguments against killing human beings in war. But they do not provide, according to Norman, an absolute moral presumption against killing, even if it is difficult for the presumption against killing to be overridden. Regan's article is, despite its title, not so much a defense of pacifism as a brilliant critique of Narveson's argument against pacifism. Regan establishes that pacifism is not necessarily false, but his own view seems to be that "extreme pacifism" (view H above *as well as* view E above?) lacks moral sensitivity to those who have received unjust violence. I hope that I have at least shown "sensitivity" to these victims even if I have not convinced those like Regan, Norman, and Teichman that E, at the very least, if not H, is defensible.

Chapter Seven

1. Henri Bergson, *The Two Sources of Morality and Religion*, trans. Brereton (New York: Holt, 1935), pp. 274–278.

2. Ibid.

3. See William Eckhardt, "Primitive Militarism," *Journal of Peace Research*, 1975, pp. 55–62; Quincy Wright, *A Study of War* (Chicago: University of Chicago Press, 1965).

4. See Arnold Toynbee, *Civilization on Trial and The World and the West* (New York: New American Library, 1976).

5. Ibid., esp. "Russia's Byzantine Heritage" and "Russia and the West."

6. Toynbee, "Russia and the West," p. 238.

7. Alfred North Whitehead, *Adventures of Ideas* (New York: Free Press, 1967), esp. "From Force to Persuasion."

8. See Joseph Kunkel, "Just War Doctrine and Pacifism," *The Thomist* 47 (Oct. 1983): 501–512.

9. See Duane Cady, "Backing Into Pacifism," *Philosophy and Social Criticism* 10 (Winter, 1984): 173–180.

10. See Kenneth Wenker, "Just War Pacifism," *Proceedings of the American Catholic Philosophical Association* 57 (1983): 135–141.

11. See Peter Beckman, Larry Campbell, Paul Crumlish, Michael Dobkowski, and Steven Lee, *The Nuclear Predicament* (Englewood Cliffs, N.J.: Prentice-Hall, 1989), p. 209.

12. See James Kellenberger, "A Defense of Pacifism," *Faith and Philosophy* 4 (Apr. 1987): 129–148, and Craig Ihara, "In Defense of a Version of Pacifism," *Ethics* 88 (July 1978): 369–374.

13. See Beckman et al., *Nuclear Predicament*, p. 211.

14. Ibid., p. 218.

15. Ibid., p. 220. It should be noted that when just war theorists and realists criticize pacifists for being "imprudent" they are relying on an attenuated definition of "prudence." The term has traditionally been connected with the moral virtue of choosing and pursuing the right means to the right end. Just as "philanthropy" now refers to giving money away so as to receive admiration from others, the attenuated version of "prudence" refers to a contriving and mean-spirited quality.

16. See my *Philosophy of Vegetarianism* (Amherst: University of Massachusetts Press, 1984).

17. Contrast Richard Routley, in "On the Alleged Inconsistency, Moral Insensitivity, and Fanaticism of Pacifism," *Inquiry* 27 (Mar. 1984): 117–136, who, although a defender of pacifism, disassociates pacifism from vegetarianism, with Rosemary Rodd, in "Pacifism and Absolute Rights for Animals," *Journal of Applied Philosophy* 2 (Mar. 1985): 53–62, who argues for similarities between the two. Also note that Jesus (although not a vegetarian) claimed that God cares even for the fall of a sparrow (Matt. 10:28).

Chapter Eight

1. See Stanley Hauerwas, "Pacifism: Some Preliminary Considerations," *Faith and Philosophy* 2 (Apr. 1985): 99–104. For a treatment of why Hartshorne, although brilliant on the connection between classical theism and violence, is not a pacifist see David Basinger, "Human Coercion: A Fly in the Process Ointment?" *Process Studies* 15 (Fall, 1986): 116–171.

2. For a fuller treatment of divine inclusiveness see my "Does God Have a Body?" *Journal of Speculative Philosophy* 2 (1988): 225–232. For a critique of analytic Thomism see my "Must a Perfect Being Be Immutable?" in Robert Kane, ed., *Hartshorne, Process Philosophy and Theology* (Albany: State University of New York Press, 1989). And on the compatibility of pacifism and mysticism see my *Journey Into the Night: A Contemporary Appreciation of Saint John of the Cross* (Albany: State University of New York Press, forthcoming).

3. See Charles Hartshorne, *Philosophers Speak of God* (Chicago: University of Chicago Press, 1953), p. 3. I have especially relied on this book.

4. See Charles Hartshorne, *Beyond Humanism* (Lincoln: University of Nebraska Press, 1968; orig. pub. 1937), pp. 26–27. Here Hartshorne notices the danger, when human beings develop a fetish for coercive power, in emulating God as tyrant. Hartshorne, however, at times flirts with just war theory by showing skepticism regarding human beings who try to settle all human affairs with love, without resort to coercive force.

5. Hartshorne's thoughts on pacifism show a remarkable consistency from *Beyond Humanism* to *Wisdom as Moderation* (Albany: State University of New York Press, 1987), p. 35. Throughout his career Hartshorne has seen strengths in pacifism, especially now that fighting war means that we risk everything; but Hartshorne also thinks that doing without war at times seems impossible. Thus, in this chapter I am trying to do a more consistent job than Hartshorne of thinking through the ethical consequences of Hartshorne's own logic of perfection, especially the idea of God's

power as a (Platonic) persuasion of the world toward goodness. Also see Charles Hartshorne, *Man's Vision of God* (New York: Harper and Brothers, 1941), pp. 166–173.

6. See Hartshorne's *The Divine Relativity* (New Haven, Conn.: Yale University Press, 1948), pp. 154–155.

7. See A. J. P. Taylor, *The Origins of the Second World War* (New York: Atheneum, 1962), p. 278. Although Taylor has had his critics (for example, Trevor-Roper), no one, as far as I know, has ever criticized him on this quotation.

8. In the remarks that follow and in the quotations from Alfred North Whitehead in this chapter I will be relying on "Peace," in *Adventures of Ideas* (New York: Free Press, 1967). Also see an excellent article by Robert Kinast, "Non-Violence in a Process Worldview," *Philosophy Today* 25 (Winter, 1981): 279–285. As is well known, the importance of Whitehead's eternal objects is trimmed somewhat by Hartshorne.

9. Whitehead, *Adventures of Ideas*, p. 381.

10. See Charles Hartshorne, "The Ethics of Contributionism," in Ernest Partridge, ed., *Responsibilities to Future Generations* (Buffalo: Prometheus, 1981), p. 105; Hartshorne, *Insights and Oversights of Great Thinkers* (Albany: State University of New York Press, 1983), pp. 183–184, 220–221, 223, 225, 228–229, 240, 244, 261, 321, 335–336; and Hartshorne, *Omnipotence and Other Theological Mistakes* (Albany: State University of New York Press, 1984), pp. 24, 86, 110, 131–133.

11. Hartshorne, *Insights and Oversights*, p. 336. Also see Hartshorne, "A Philosophy of Democratic Defense," in Bryson and Finkelstein, ed., *Science, Philosophy, and Religion*, Second Symposium (New York, 1942), pp. 130–172; Hartshorne, *Reality as Social Process* (Boston: Beacon, 1953), pp. 213–219; Hartshorne, "The Unity of Man and the Unity of Nature," in Hartshorne, *The Logic of Perfection* (LaSalle, Ill.: Open Court, 1962), pp. 298–299; and Hartshorne, *Creative Synthesis and Philosophic Method* (LaSalle, Ill.: Open Court, 1970), pp. 308, 320.

12. See Carl Jung, *Answer to Job* (Princeton, N.J.: Princeton University Press, 1972), although Jung does not move, as I would,

to pacifism once the moral inferiority of the character of God in the last book of the Bible is exposed.

13. See Paul Kuntz, "Whitehead the Anglican and Russell the Puritan: The Traditional Origins of Muddleheadedness and Simplemindedness," *Process Studies* 17 (Spring, 1988): 40–44.

14. Sidney Axinn, *A Moral Military* (Philadelphia: Temple University Press, 1989).

15. See Duane Cady, *From Warism to Pacifism: A Moral Continuum* (Philadelphia: Temple University Press, 1989). Also see James Turner Johnson's *The Quest for Peace* (Princeton, N.J.: Princeton University Press, 1987), where Johnson distinguishes between sectarian pacifism of withdrawal from the world and utopian world-perfecting pacifism, the latter of which aims at establishing a more rightly constituted political order.

16. Robert Holmes, *On War and Morality* (Princeton, N.J.: Princeton University Press, 1988).

17. Cf. the criticisms of recent pacifism in Guenter Lewy, *Peace and Revolution: The Moral Crisis of American Pacifism* (Grand Rapids, Mich.: Eerdmans, 1988).

Epilogue

1. George Weigel, *Tranquillitas Ordinis: The Present Failure and Future Promise of American Catholic Thought on War and Peace* (Oxford: Oxford University Press, 1987).

2. Ibid., p. 391.

3. Ibid., pp. 87, 183.

4. Ibid., p. 210.

5. Ibid., p. 343.

6. Ibid., p. 30.

7. Ibid., pp. 36–38, 188.

8. Ibid., p. 41, no. 5.

9. Ibid.

10. Ibid., p. 125.

11. Ibid., pp. 127, 183, 282.

12. Ibid., p. 382.

13. Ibid., p. 383.

14. Ibid., pp. 260, 264.

15. Ibid., p. 350.

16. Ibid., p. 144.

17. Ibid., p. 102.

18. Ibid., pp. 277–278, 381.

19. Ibid., pp. 145, 330.

20. Ibid., p. 349.

21. Ibid., p. 360.

22. Ibid., p. 369.

23. Ibid., p. 383.

24. Ibid., p. 377.

25. Ibid., p. 378.

26. Ibid., pp. 194–195.

27. Ibid., p. 189.

28. Ibid., p. 196.

29. Ibid., pp. 208, 380.

30. Ibid., p. 378.

31. Ibid., p. 393.

32. For example, Berrigan was prevented from speaking by the university administration at Saint Joseph's University in Philadelphia in 1981.

33. Weigel, *Tranquillitas Ordinis*, p. 229.

34. Ibid., p. 232.

35. Ibid., p. 135.

36. James Schall, "Ecclesiastical Wars Over Peace," *National Review* 34 (June 25, 1982).

37. William O'Brien, *The Conduct of Just and Limited War* (New York: Praeger, 1981); George Mavrodes, "Conventions and the Morality of War," *Philosophy and Public Affairs* 4 (1975): 117–131; Joseph Nye, *Nuclear Ethics* (New York: Free Press, 1986), pp. 57–58, 114–115.

38. "The French Bishops' Statement: Winning Peace," *Origins* 13 (Dec. 8, 1983): 443.

39. G. R. Dunstan, "Theological Method in the Deterrence Debate," in Geoffrey L. Goodwin, ed., *Ethics and Nuclear Deter-*

rence (London: Croom Helm, 1982), p. 50; Michael Novak, *Moral Clarity in the Nuclear Age* (New York: Nelson, 1983), pp. 60–61.

40. Trent, Session VI, canon 19 (1547).

41. W. D. Ross, *The Right and the Good* (Oxford: Clarendon, 1930), pp. 22, 61, 64. Also see Michael Walzer's chapter titled "Supreme Emergency" in *Just and Unjust Wars* (New York: Basic Books, 1977).

42. Roh's views are treated in Henry Davis, *Moral and Pastoral Theology* (London: Sheed and Ward, 1943), p. 247. For Ford, see John Ford, "The Morality of Obliteration Bombing," *Theological Studies* 5 (1944): 261–309.

43. John Finnis, Joseph Boyle, and Germain Grisez, *Nuclear Deterrence, Morality and Realism* (Oxford: Clarendon Press, 1987).

44. Ibid., p. 78.

45. Ibid., p. 79.

46. Ibid., p. 89.

47. Ibid., p. 92.

48. Ibid., p. 136.

49. Ibid., p. 160, et al.

50. Ibid., pp. 150–151.

51. Ibid., p. 186.

52. Gregory Kavka, "Deterrence, Utility, and Rational Choice," *Theory and Decision* 12 (1980): 52–56.

53. Finnis, Boyle, and Grisez, *Nuclear Deterrence*, p. 208.

54. Ibid., p. 209.

55. This thesis is opposed by Jeff McMahan, "Nuclear Deterrence and Future Generations," in Avner Cohen and Steven Lee, eds., *Nuclear Weapons and the Future of Humanity* (Totowa, N.J.: Rowman and Allenheld, 1986), pp. 323, 330.

56. Finnis, Boyle, and Grisez, *Nuclear Deterrence*, pp. 220, 225.

57. Ibid., p. 251.

58. Ibid., pp. 144, 147.

59. Ibid., p. 358.

60. Cf. Kenneth Himes, "Deterrence and Disarmament: Ethical Evaluation and Pastoral Advice," *Cross Currents* 33 (1983–1984): 421–431; David Hollenbach, *Nuclear Ethics: A Christian Moral Argument* (New York: Paulist Press, 1983), p. 71, who thinks that

deterrence is needed to protect *our* innocents; and Barrie Paskins, "Deep Cuts Are Morally Imperative," in Goodwin, ed., *Ethics and Nuclear Deterrence*, pp. 99–100.

61. Finnis, Boyle, and Grisez, *Nuclear Deterrence*, p. 326.
62. Ibid., p. viii.
63. Ibid., p. 65.
64. Ibid., p. 67.
65. Ibid., p. 132.
66. Ibid., pp. 353–354.
67. Ibid., p. 106.
68. Ibid., pp. 310–312.
69. Ibid., p. 316.
70. Ibid., p. 332.
71. Ibid., p. 338.

BIBLIOGRAPHY

This bibliography is divided into two parts. The first is an annotated listing of sources for those who wish to pursue studies in
Christian pacifism. The second lists the works cited in this book.

Studies in Christian Pacifism

Bainton, Roland. *Christian Attitudes Toward War and Peace: A
Historical Survey and Critical Evaluation.* Nashville: Abing-
ton, 1960. Bainton's work traces the ideals of peace in antiquity through the pacifism of the early church to the just
war to the crusades to recent concepts of war from Waterloo
to Armageddon. Pacifism is favorably treated throughout.

Cadoux, C. John. *The Early Christian Attitude to War: A Contri-
bution to the History of Christian Ethics.* New York: Seabury,
1982. Originally published in 1919, this classic study details
the teaching of Jesus, the forms of early Christian disapproval
of war, and then the forms of Christian acceptance of war,
as well as the bearing of early Christian views on "modern"
conditions.

Douglass, James. *The Non-Violent Cross: A Theology of Revolution and Peace.* New York: Macmillan, 1968. Douglass provides a defense of pacifism in an age where the world is seen

as crucifixion. Vatican II is treated in detail, as are Dietrich Bonhoeffer, Gandhi, and Jesus. An effort is made to understand the implications of a non-violent revolution for history and politics.

Hauerwas, Stanley. *Against the Nations: War and Survival in a Liberal Society*. Minneapolis: Winston, 1985. Dedicated to Paul Ramsey (a just war theorist) and John Yoder (a pacifist), this book confronts the challenge of the Holocaust with an attempt to survive justly. The elimination of war is viewed as a theological imperative.

James, William. "The Moral Equivalent of War." In Richard A. Wasserstrom, ed., *War and Morality*. Los Angeles: Wadsworth, 1970. Originally published in 1910, this is an attempt to bolster pacifism by giving it the virtues traditionally associated with the military—discipline, devotion to a cause, courage, and the like—so as to trim the flab off pacifism. In short, James wants to establish a moral equivalent to war.

Kinast, Robert. "Non-Violence in a Process Worldview." *Philosophy Today* 25 (Winter, 1981): 279–285. Kinast's work is an attempt to show that the God described by process thinkers helps us to understand peace better—better, that is, than in the traditional view of God—and an attempt to claim that pacifism offers us a more direct and intense avenue to the eternal object "Peace" than other options.

McSorley, Richard. *New Testament Basis of Peacemaking*. Scottdale, Pa.: Herald, 1985. This defense of pacifism through the New Testament treats the familiar New Testament texts often used to support war, as well as the familiar objections to pacifism. The American Catholic bishops' statement on war and peace is also discussed.

Merton, Thomas. *Thomas Merton on Peace*. New York: McCall, 1971. Although Merton did not consider himself a pacifist, many have been "converted" to pacifism because of his insightful, meditative, and persuasive essays on Christian peace.

Musto, Ronald. *The Catholic Peace Tradition*. New York: Orbis, 1986. This monumental work details every period in the history of Catholicism, from the first century to the twentieth. Serious students will read all of this, but the work can also be used profitably as a reference work.

Whitehead, Alfred North. "From Force to Persuasion" and "Peace." In Whitehead, *Adventures of Ideas*, pp. 69–86, 284–298. New York: Free Press, 1967. Originally published in 1933, these essays are attempts to accomplish the goal of peace in a civilized society. Whitehead sees peace as nonetheless inclusive of tragedy in life and as compatible with God's attributes.

Yoder, John. *The Politics of Jesus*. Grand Rapids, Mich.: Eerdmans, 1972. The Gospel texts, especially Luke, are examined and then applied to the life of the apostolic community. The conclusions support a type of pacifism and theologically based radicalism and proclaim the relevance of the incarnation for social life today; the coin for Caesar is examined in detail.

———. *What Would You Do? A Serious Answer to a Standard Question*. Scottdale, Pa.: Herald, 1983. Yoder analyzes the assumptions behind the question "What would you do?" (for example, What would you do if someone attacked your grandmother?) as well as various responses from pacifists—for example, Tolstoy. The practicality of such responses is also considered in detail.

Zahn, Gordon. *War, Conscience, and Dissent*. New York: Hawthorn, 1967. This is an examination of modern war and the Christian by a pacifist; private conscience and dissent within the state and the church are treated, particularly within the German state under Hitler.

Works Cited

Ansbro, John. *Martin Luther King, Jr.: The Making of a Mind*. Maryknoll, N.Y.: Orbis, 1982.

Anscombe, G. E. M. "War and Murder." In James Rachels, ed., *Moral Problems*, 3rd ed. New York: Harper and Row, 1979. Also in Anscombe's *Collected Philosophical Papers*. Minneapolis: University of Minnesota Press, 1981.

Aquinas, Saint Thomas. *Summa Contra Gentiles*. Pegis ed. Garden City, N.Y.: Image, 1957.

———. *Summa Theologiae*. Blackfriars ed. New York: McGraw-Hill, 1972.

Augustine, Saint. *Epistle 138 to Marcellinus, Contra Faustum,* and *Epistle 189 to Boniface*.

Axinn, Sidney. *A Moral Military*. Philadelphia: Temple University Press, 1989.

Basinger, David. "Human Coercion: A Fly in the Process Ointment?" *Process Studies* 15 (Fall, 1986): 161–171.

Beckman, Peter, Larry Campbell, Paul Crumlish, Michael Dobkowski, and Steven Lee. *The Nuclear Predicament*. Englewood Cliffs, N.J.: Prentice-Hall, 1989.

Bergson, Henri. *The Two Sources of Morality and Religion*, trans. Brereton. New York: Holt, 1935.

Brock, Peter. *Pacifism in Europe to 1914*. Princeton, N.J.: Princeton University Press, 1972.

———. *Twentieth Century Pacifism*. New York: Van Nostrand, 1976.

Cady, Duane. "Backing into Pacifism." *Philosophy and Social Criticism* 10 (Winter, 1984): 173–180.

———. *From Warism to Pacifism: A Moral Continuum*. Philadelphia: Temple University Press, 1989.

Childress, James. "Just-War Criteria." In Thomas Shannon, ed., *War or Peace? The Search for New Answers*. Maryknoll, N.Y.: Orbis, 1980.

Dunstan, G. R. "Theological Method in the Deterrence Debate." In Geoffrey L. Goodwin, ed., *Ethics and Nuclear Deterrence*. London: Croom Helm, 1982.

Eckhardt, William. "Primitive Militarism." *Journal of Peace Research*, 1975, pp. 55–62.

Finnis, John, Joseph Boyle, and Germain Grisez. *Nuclear Deterrence, Morality and Realism*. Oxford: Clarendon, 1987.

Ford, John. "The Morality of Obliteration Bombing." *Theological Studies* 5 (1944): 261–309. Also in Richard A. Wasserstrom, ed., *War and Morality*. Los Angeles: Wadsworth, 1970.

"The French Bishops' Statement: Winning Peace." *Origins* 13 (Dec. 8, 1983).

Gandhi, M. K. *Non-Violence in Peace and War*. Navajivan, 1949.

Hauerwas, Stanley. "Pacifism: Some Preliminary Considerations." *Faith and Philosophy* 2 (Apr. 1985): 99–104.

Himes, Kenneth. "Deterrence and Disarmament: Ethical Evaluation and Pastoral Advice." *Cross Currents* 33 (1983–1984): 421–431.

Hollenbach, David. *Nuclear Ethics: A Christian Moral Argument*. New York: Paulist Press, 1983.

Holmes, Robert. *On War and Morality*. Princeton, N.J.: Princeton University Press, 1988.

Ihara, Craig. "In Defense of a Version of Pacifism." *Ethics* 88 (July 1978): 369–374.

Iyer, Raghavan. *The Moral and Political Thought of Mahatma Gandhi*. Oxford: Oxford University Press, 1973.

Johnson, James Turner. *Ideology, Reason, and the Limitations of War: Religious and Secular Concepts, 1200–1740*. Princeton, N.J.: Princeton University Press, 1975.

————. *Just War Tradition and the Restraint of War: A Moral and Historical Inquiry*. Princeton, N.J.: Princeton University Press, 1981.

————. *Can Modern War Be Just?* New Haven, Conn.: Yale University Press, 1984.

————. "Historical Tradition and Moral Judgment: The Case of Just War Tradition." *Journal of Religion* 64 (1984): 299–317.

————. *The Quest for Peace*. Princeton, N.J.: Princeton University Press, 1987.

Kant, Immanuel. "Perpetual Peace." In L. W. Beck, ed., *On History*. Indianapolis: Bobbs-Merrill, 1963.

Kavka, Gregory. "Deterrence, Utility, and Rational Choice." *Theory and Decision* 12 (1980): 52–56.

Kellenberger, James. "A Defense of Pacifism." *Faith and Philosophy* 4 (Apr. 1987): 129–148.

Kennan, George F. *The Nuclear Delusion*. New York: Pantheon, 1983.

Kissinger, Henry. "Force and Diplomacy in the Nuclear Age." *Foreign Affairs*, Apr. 1956.

Kunkel, Joseph. "Just War Doctrine and Pacifism." *The Thomist* 47 (Oct. 1983): 501–512.

Kuntz, Paul. "Whitehead the Anglican and Russell the Puritan: The Traditional Origins of Muddleheadedness and Simple-mindedness." *Process Studies* 17 (Spring, 1988): 40–44.

Lackey, Douglas. *The Ethics of War and Peace.* Englewood Cliffs, N.J.: Prentice-Hall, 1989.

Lewy, Guenter. *Peace and Revolution: The Moral Crisis of American Pacifism.* Grand Rapids, Mich.: Eerdmans, 1988.

McMahan, Jeff. "Nuclear Deterrence and Future Generations." In Avner Cohen and Steven Lee, ed., *Nuclear Weapons and the Future of Humanity.* Totowa, N.J.: Rowman and Allenheld, 1986.

Martin, Michael. "On an Argument Against Pacifism." *Philosophical Studies* 26 (Dec. 1974): 437–442.

Mavrodes, George. "Conventions and the Morality of War." *Philosophy and Public Affairs* 4 (1975): 117–131.

Morgenthau, Hans. *Politics Among Nations.* New York: Knopf, 1949.

Nagel, Thomas. "Ruthlessness in Public Life." In Stuart Hampshire, ed., *Public and Private Morality.* Cambridge, Eng.: Cambridge University Press, 1978.

National Conference of Catholic Bishops, *The Challenge of Peace: God's Promise and Our Response.* Washington, D.C., May 3, 1983.

Norman, Richard. "The Case for Pacifism." *Journal of Applied Philosophy* 5 (1988): 197–210.

Novak, Michael. *Moral Clarity in the Nuclear Age.* New York: Nelson, 1983.

Nye, Joseph. *Nuclear Ethics.* New York: Free Press, 1986.

O'Brien, William. *The Conduct of Just and Limited War.* New York: Praeger, 1981.

Paskins, Barrie. "Deep Cuts Are Morally Imperative." In Geoffrey L. Goodwin, ed., *Ethics and Nuclear Deterrence.* London: Croom Helm, 1982.

Plato. *The Collected Dialogues of Plato*, ed. Hamilton and Cairns. Princeton, N.J.: Princeton University Press, 1973. Greek edition ed. Burnet.

Ramsey, Paul. *War and the Christian Conscience*. Durham, N.C.: Duke University Press, 1961.

———. *The Just War*. New York: Scribner's, 1968.

Regan, Tom. "A Defense of Pacifism." *Canadian Journal of Philosophy* 2 (Sept. 1972): 73–86.

Rodd, Rosemary. "Pacifism and Absolute Rights for Animals." *Journal of Applied Philosophy* 2 (Mar. 1985): 53–62.

Ross, W. D. *The Right and the Good*. Oxford: Clarendon, 1930.

Routley, Richard. "On the Alleged Inconsistency, Moral Insensitivity, and Fanaticism of Pacifism." *Inquiry* 27 (Mar. 1984): 117–136.

Russell, Frederick. *The Just War in the Middle Ages*. Cambridge, Eng.: Cambridge University Press, 1975.

Schall, James. "Ecclesiastical Wars Over Peace." *National Review* 34 (June 25, 1982).

Sharp, Gene. *Exploring Nonviolent Alternatives*. Boston: Porter Sargent, 1971.

Steinkraus, Warren. "Does It Make Any Sense to Talk About a 'Just War'?" *Journal of Social Philosophy* 5 (Jan. 1974): 8–11.

Sterba, James. "How to Achieve Nuclear Deterrence Without Threatening Nuclear Destruction." In Sterba, ed., *The Ethics of War and Nuclear Deterrence*, pp. 155–168. Los Angeles: Wadsworth, 1985.

Taylor, A. J. P. *The Origins of the Second World War*. New York: Atheneum, 1962.

Teichman, Jenny. *Pacifism and the Just War*. New York: Blackwell, 1986.

Toynbee, Arnold. *Civilization on Trial and The World and the West*. New York: New American Library, 1976.

United Methodist Council of Bishops. *In Defense of Creation*. Nashville: Graded Press, 1986.

Urmson, J. O. "Saints and Heroes." In A. I. Melden, ed., *Essays in Moral Philosophy*, pp. 198–216. Seattle: University of Washington Press, 1958.

Vanderpol, Alfred. *La doctrine scholastique du droit de guerre.* Paris: Pedone, 1919.

Walzer, Michael. *Just and Unjust Wars.* New York: Basic Books, 1977.

Wasserstrom, Richard A. "On the Morality of War: A Preliminary Inquiry." In Wasserstrom, ed., *War and Morality*, pp. 78–101. Los Angeles: Wadsworth, 1970.

Weigel, George. "The Catholics and the Arms Race: A Primer for the Perplexed." *Chicago Studies* 18 (1979): 169–195.

———. *Tranquillitas Ordinis: The Present Failure and Future Promise of American Catholic Thought on War and Peace.* Oxford: Oxford University Press, 1987.

Wells, Donald. *War Crimes and Laws of War.* Lanham, Md.: University Press of America, 1984.

Wenker, Kenneth. "Just War Pacifism." *Proceedings of the American Catholic Philosophical Association* 57 (1983): 135–141.

Wright, Quincy. *A Study of War.* Chicago: University of Chicago Press, 1965.

INDEX OF NAMES

179

Index

Eisenhower, Dwight, 139
El Greco, 59, 156n.2, 157nn.5,6

Feuerbach, Ludwig, 121
Finnis, John, xi, 142–147
Ford, John, 142, 152n.5, 169n.42
Francis of Assisi, Saint, 32, 59, 70, 73–74, 77, 123
Franco, Francisco, 110

Gandhi, M. K., x, xii, 52, 72–74, 76–81, 83–84, 94, 109, 123–124, 131, 158n.22
Giordano, Luca, 60, 157n.11
Giotto, 58
Grisez, Germain, xi, 142–147
Grotius, Hugo, 40

Harris, Arthur, 54
Hartshorne, Charles, 116, 120, 127–128, 165nn.3, 4, 5, 166nn.6, 10, 11
Hauerwas, Stanley, 115, 160n.4
Hegel, G. W. F., 79
Heraclitus, 79
Hesburgh, Theodore, 137
Himes, Kenneth, 169n.60
Hitler, Adolph, 5, 47, 123–124
Hobbes, Thomas, 25, 45, 99, 106
Ho Chi Minh, 140
Hollenbach, David, 169n.60
Holmes, Robert, 130
Homer, 57
Hunthausen, Raymond, 38

Iyer, Raghavan, 72–73

James, William, 161n.5
Jesus, x, xii, 3–4, 6–10, 12–21, 28, 32, 36, 38, 51, 55–62, 65, 67, 70, 74, 77, 80, 123, 151n.9, 159n.31, 164n.17
Johnson, James Turner, x, 31–37, 160n.4, 167n.15

Johnson, Lyndon, 141
John the Baptist, 8–9, 12
John XXIII, Pope, 137
Jouvenet, Jean Baptiste, 60
Jung, Carl, 128, 166n.12

Kahn, Herman, 144
Kant, Immanuel, xii, 23, 53–54, 75, 77, 79–80, 85, 94, 106, 128, 142, 149n.2, 150n.7, 163n.36
Karenina, Anna, 101
Kavka, Gregory, 144
Kazantzakis, Nikos, 152n.1
Kellenberger, James, 164n.12
Kennan, George F., 27, 30, 91–92, 145
Keynes, John Maynard, 124
Kierkegaard, Søren, 73
Kinast, Robert, 166n.8
King, Martin Luther Jr., x, xii, 52, 66, 78–81, 84, 94, 123, 131
King Khaled, 104
Kissinger, Henry, 159n.33
Kolbe, Maximillian, 71
Krol, John, 137
Krushchev, Nikita, 109
Kuhn, Thomas, 17
Kunkel, Joseph, 164n.8
Kuntz, Paul, 129

Lackey, Douglas, x, 80–85, 99, 159n.33, 160n.49
Lewy, Guenter, 167n.17
Lincoln, Abraham, 128

McMahan, Jeff, 169n.55
Malchus, 4, 8, 10
Malik-al-Kamil, 70
Martin, Michael, 161n.11
Marx, Karl, 79, 135
Mavrodes, George, 141, 160n.44
Merton, Thomas, 94
Mill, John Stuart, xii, 72
Miller, Arthur, 130, 159n.31